The Classroom is a Stage

Carlos Gontow

The Classroom is a Stage

40 short plays for English students

DISAL
EDITORA

Coordenação editorial
Paulo Nascimento Verano

Leitura crítica
Ethan Talmage e Cris Gontow

Capa e projeto gráfico
Paula Astiz

Editoração eletrônica
Paula Astiz Design

Dados Internacionais de Catalogação na Publicação (CIP)
(Câmara Brasileira do Livro, SP, Brasil)

Gontow, Carlos
The classroom is a stage : 40 short plays for English students / Carlos Gontow. – São Paulo : Disal, 2005.

ISBN 85-89533-29-8

1. Inglês – Estudo e ensino I. Título.

05-3095 CDD-420.7

Índices para catálogo sistemático:
1. Inglês : Estudo e ensino 420.7

DISAL EDITORA

Rua Major Sertório, 771, cj. 1, Vila Buarque
01222-001, São Paulo, SP
Tel./Fax: (11) 3237-0070

Visite nosso site: www.disaleditora.com.br

Vendas:
Televendas: (11) 3226-3111
Fax gratuito: 0800 7707 105/106
E-mail para pedidos: comercialdisal@disal.com.br

Table of Contents

Introduction
An Interview with the Author

CHARACTERS *A reporter from the New York Times*
Carlos Gontow, the author of "The Classroom is a Stage"

(Carlos is walking down the street. The reporter approaches him.)

REPORTER Excuse me, sir. I'm a reporter from "The New York Times."

CARLOS *(With a smile.)* Yes?

REPORTER You're Carlos Gontow, the writer of the book "The Classroom is a Stage," right?

CARLOS *(Proud.)* Yes, that's me.

REPORTER Can I ask you some questions?

CARLOS *(Trying to be nice, because "The New York Times" is a famous newspaper.)* Sure. Go ahead.

REPORTER You're an English teacher and an actor, right?

CARLOS That's right.

REPORTER How long have you been an English teacher?

CARLOS Since 1987.

REPORTER And why did you decide to use theater to teach English?

CARLOS *(Thinks for a while.)* Well, uh... I don't exactly know. I've always loved theater and ever since I was a young boy in school, I've always used theater in my presentations.

REPORTER What do you mean?

CARLOS When I was in school and I had to present a paper on something, let's say the discovery of America, I would put on a little play and tell the story in theater form. It was fun, and students who watched it had fun, too and learned a lot. So for me it was only natural to use theater to teach English.

REPORTER And what are the advantages of using theater to learn English?

CARLOS There are many advantages. *(Thinks.)* Uh... First of all, theater recreates life, and the language used in theater is very close to the language we use in real life. In real life, people hesitate... uh... make mistakes, forget what they were going to say... let me see... what else?... Well, they misunderstand each other, leave unfinished sentences, are interrupted by others... uh... I think that's it... Language in textbooks is "too perfect"...

REPORTER *(Interrupting.)* Too perfect?

CARLOS Yeah, one line follows another without interruptions. You know exactly what the other person is going to say. Many times students have the feeling that they have to memorize the conversations in their textbooks and get frustrated when they are not able to follow them perfectly. In real life, there are many different ways to say the same thing, and you cannot control what the other person is going to say. You have to be ready to improvise.

REPORTER But in theater you know what the other person is going to say. Don't you have to memorize the... the... what's it called?

CARLOS The script.

REPORTER Yes... sorry... don't actors have to memorize the script?

CARLOS Of course they do, but many times people forget the script, change words, use a synonym instead of the word that's written in the text. They have to improvise. And in real life they have to improvise, too. So this experience will prepare them for life.

REPORTER That's interesting.

CARLOS And in real life, when people communicate, they use gestures, facial expressions, body language, eye contact... uh... many other features of communication. In a classroom, many times students read a dialog looking at the book. They don't communicate to each other. They don't change the tones of their voices. They read the dialogs mechanically. That is very artificial.

REPORTER And what other advantages are there?

CARLOS Well, theater can increase students' motivation.

REPORTER How?

CARLOS Many students, especially young ones, learn English because their parents force them to. A lot of English students don't have a chance to travel to English speaking countries or speak to native speakers and never get a chance to put what they are learning into practice. It's common to see English students ask, "Why do I have to study English?" Parents say, "English is important for your future." But for them the future is tonight. They can't relate to an objective that is so far away from them. When we are rehearsing a play, they only think about the presentation of the play. They have to learn their lines and act them out well, because they want to look good on stage. They have an objective in mind when they come to the English class, "I have to study English to present this play." They'll really look forward to presenting it. And they learn English much faster when they're motivated. And most of all, theater is fun!

REPORTER Fun?

CARLOS *(Smiles.)* Sure! It's fun to pretend to be somebody else and say and do many things that you don't do in your everyday life. I like to say to my students that being an actor is not being afraid of the ridiculous. You can be ridiculous, you can say ridiculous things, because you are not you – you are the character you are playing.

REPORTER And how about grammar? Do students learn grammar when they're acting?

CARLOS Theater is a wonderful way to help students to learn structures. When they're acting, they don't think about grammar – they just worry about remembering their lines and acting. By repeating the same lines many times, they will eventually remember them and, consequently, acquire lots of grammar structures. And a funny thing that happens is that, at the end, all students know everybody's lines, so they learn much more.

REPORTER I see. So how can teachers use the plays in your book?

CARLOS Well, there are 40 short plays – sketches – in the book. Before each sketch there's a page with some information for teachers – the level of English, the grammar structures and vocabulary involved in the sketch, the recommended age for the students, the number of characters (with some suggestions to change it), suggestions for costumes, the playing time and some suggestions for production. It's very easy to find a play that is good for your students. And you can always adapt the stories.

REPORTER How?

CARLOS I included two plays, "Mr. Ache" and "The Rabbit Family Game," which have different versions, with more or fewer characters, and more difficult or easier lines. They're two examples of what teachers can do with all the plays – change them, include more things, omit things. Everything is possible. There are some sketches that were inspired by other plays and books, and I really hope teachers will be inspired to write or adapt their own sketches.

REPORTER If teachers don't want to put on a show or simply don't have time to rehearse a play, can they still use your book?

CARLOS Definitely! All the sketches can be done in the classroom, with very simple scenery and props. That's why the book is called "The Classroom is a Stage." You don't need a theater to use these plays. Teachers can simply have students read the plays in small groups. Students can present them in front of the class, just reading their lines. Teachers should encourage students to stand up, move, look at each other, touch each other, and raise their voices. They can also ask students to read a play and write a different version of the same story. Students can write it at home, then rehearse in class and present it at the end.

REPORTER What else?

CARLOS Well, they can always put on a show – a combination of many sketches – and present it. Parents love to see their children acting and speaking English on stage. You can do it as an extra-class activity and get students from different classes to put on a play and present it to the whole school. In this case, you can get students who don't want to act to be sound operators, backstage assistants, costume designers, or anything you can think of. You can have a school festival and have groups from different classes present their plays. There are so many possibilities!

REPORTER Do you have any suggestions for teachers who want to put on a play with their students?

CARLOS Let me think... Uh... Practice it many times, help the students to remember their lines, show them their positions on stage. At the end of each rehearsal, have them do the whole play without any interruptions. This will help them to get confidence. Tell them to continue even if they make a mistake.

REPORTER Why?

CARLOS Because mistakes happen and they have to be ready to improvise. Also, when students are presenting the play, don't help them and don't stay on stage with them.

REPORTER Why not?

CARLOS I think teachers who help the students all the time or stay on stage with them while they're doing the play are sending them the message, "I don't think you can do it." It's important to trust your students and make them feel confident. Rehearse the play as many times as necessary, stop when you have to correct them, do it again and again and again. Then do it once from beginning to end, without any interruptions or corrections. Tell them that this is what's going to happen when they're presenting the show. When the rehearsal is over, you can make comments like, "You forgot to say this," "You've said the wrong lines," "You have to stand a little bit to the left," etc.

REPORTER Don't students feel bad when they make a mistake?

CARLOS It's OK to make mistakes. Everybody makes mistakes. I also like to tell my students that the audience doesn't know what they're supposed to say, so if they make a mistake, it's OK. Of course we should try to correct all the mistakes during rehearsals. If students get used to the fact that you won't help them, they will study their parts better and, as a result, will be more confident on stage. Otherwise, they'll always depend on the teachers.

REPORTER I understand. Any other suggestions?

CARLOS Speak English all the time when you're rehearsing the play and tell the students to do the same. This will also help students to be more fluent and ready for improvisations if something goes wrong.

REPORTER Mr. Gontow...

CARLOS *(Interrupting him.)* Call me Carlos, please.

REPORTER Carlos, are the plays in this book only for children?

CARLOS No, definitely not. There are many plays that can be used by teenagers and adults. I find, from my experience, that adult students love to role play and act. They have a great time rehearsing a play and presenting it, even if it's just a one-day activity and if they only present it in front of the class.

REPORTER Great! Is there anything else you'd like to add?

CARLOS Uh... I just would like to thank some people who have worked with me and have helped me to write some of the plays. Let's see... Cláudia Martins, Maria Amélia Marcus, Mila Rey and Cris Gontow. And also all the students who have acted in my plays – they've learned a lot from theater and I've learned a lot from them. I'd like to dedicate this book to my wife Cris, who gives me love and inspiration, and to my kids, Bruna and Pedro.

REPORTER Well, thanks a lot for the interview.

CARLOS Oh, you're welcome. It was a pleasure.

REPORTER Bye.

CARLOS Bye... *(Calling, showing the book.)* Hey, I have a copy of the book right here. Don't you want my autograph?

REPORTER No, thanks. *(Tries to leave.)*

CARLOS *(Calling.)* How about my picture? Don't you want to take my picture? *(Dreaming, talking to himself.)* Imagine that... *my* picture in "The New York Times..." Wow!

(The reporter exits quickly, while Carlos is daydreaming.)

THE END

This book is photocopiable. Teachers can make copies of the plays they want to use and distribute them to students.

Este livro é fotocopiável para uso em sala de aula. O professor poderá fazer cópias das peças com as quais irá trabalhar e distribuí-las aos seus alunos.

An Acting Class

LEVEL OF ENGLISH: Lower intermediate

RECOMMENDED AGE: Teenagers and adults

STRUCTURES:

Grammar: Difference between "each other" and "oneself"
Vocabulary: acting vocabulary (rehearse, memorize, script, etc.)

NUMBER OF CHARACTERS: 3 – A teacher and 2 students

COSTUMES: Ordinary clothes

PLAYING TIME: Approximately 5 minutes

SOME SUGGESTIONS:

✹ You don't need special scenery for this sketch, since it's an acting class. The characters are in a classroom.
✹ It's important that the two students act very badly when they're doing the scene from the play "Goodbye my Love." The more they exaggerate, the funnier it will be.

An Acting Class[1]

CHARACTERS *Teacher*
Rick, an acting student who hates Grace
Grace, an acting student who hates Rick

(Rick and Grace are in the classroom. The teacher arrives.)

TEACHER OK, Rick and Grace. Are you ready to start our acting class?

RICK Yes.

GRACE I'm ready.

TEACHER All right. Let's start at the beginning. Let's try to rehearse the scene.

RICK Rehearse?

TEACHER Yes, rehearse, practice the scene. Actors always rehearse before they present a show. Don't you know that?

RICK Of course I do.

TEACHER Did you memorize the script I gave you last class?

GRACE Script? What's a script?

TEACHER The script is the text of the play or the film. It has the lines you have to say. Did you study the scene?

GRACE I studied *my* part. But I'm sure he didn't memorize *his* part, as usual.

RICK Of course I did.

GRACE Let's see.

TEACHER OK. OK... Let's start. This is a scene from the play "Goodbye my Love." *(To Rick.)* Rick, you are David, a doctor who takes care of poor people. *(To Grace.)* Grace, you are Jane, a nurse in India. David and Jane love each other.

1. Inspired by the story "Together Again," in the book "American Streamline Connections."

GRACE They love each other?

TEACHER Yes, they love each other. David loves Jane, and Jane loves David. They love each other.

GRACE I understand.

TEACHER Start!

(Rick and Grace act badly.)

RICK It's time too say goodbye, Jane.

GRACE Oh, no, David!

RICK I have to go.

GRACE *(Cries.)* Don't go. I love you, David.

RICK I love you, too, Jane. But I can't stay. There are many people in the world who need my help.

GRACE I know. *(Cries.)* Will we see each other again?

RICK Of course we will, Jane, because we love each other!

TEACHER Stop! Look, Grace, I know you don't like Rick and Rick, I know you don't like Grace.

GRACE Like? We hate each other!

TEACHER Yes, but you are studying to be actors. Remember that when you are acting, you are not yourselves. You are the characters. In this scene David and Jane love each other, right?

RICK Right, but...

TEACHER No "buts." You have to look at each other *(Rick and Grace look at each other with disgust.)*, you have to touch each other *(Rick and Grace touch each other's hands with disgust.)*, smile at each other *(Rick and Grace smile at each other with disgust.)*, and kiss each other. Right?

GRACE Right! I'm doing my part well, but Rick only thinks about himself.

RICK What about her? She thinks she's the best. She only talks about herself.

(Rick and Grace start talking to themselves.)

TEACHER What did you say?

RICK Nothing. I'm just talking to myself.

GRACE Me too. I'm talking to myself.

TEACHER This is theater. You're not supposed to talk to yourselves. You're supposed to talk to each other.

RICK Right, but...

TEACHER Enough. Let's start the scene again.

(They start the scene again.)

RICK It's time to say goodbye, Jane.

GRACE Oh, no, David!

RICK I have to go.

TEACHER *(Interrupting.)* Stop! Stop! Rick, let's think about this scene.

RICK Think about the scene?

TEACHER Yes. Let's think about it. If you understand what David is feeling, you'll be able to concentrate.

RICK OK.

TEACHER Rick, this is a love story. How does David feel?

RICK He's sad, because he has to go, but he doesn't want to. He loves Jane.

TEACHER Exactly, very good. We're starting to understand each other. I'm starting to understand you and you're starting to understand me. And we're starting to understand something.

RICK *(Happy.)* Good.

TEACHER Now try to show your feelings!

RICK *(Insecure.)* That's difficult...

(Grace laughs. Rick looks at her angrily.)

TEACHER Why don't you try it, Grace?

GRACE No problem. Watch this, Rick. *(Starts.)* It's time to say goodbye.

TEACHER Yes, that's right.

GRACE *(Happy.)* Did you like it?

TEACHER No, but it's really time to say goodbye. *(Looks at his watch.)* The class is over. See you next time! Bye!

(Teacher exits. Rick and Grace look at each other angrily and exit to different sides.)

THE END

At the Bookstore

LEVEL OF ENGLISH: Basic

RECOMMENDED AGE: Teenagers and adults

STRUCTURES:

Grammar: Simple present tense
Vocabulary: Homophones (Words that sound the same but are written differently)

NUMBER OF CHARACTERS: 2 – A clerk and a customer

COSTUMES: Ordinary Clothes

PLAYING TIME: Between 5 and 8 minutes

SOME SUGGESTIONS:

✷ To set the scene for the bookstore, get a bookcase and fill it with books.
✷ You can use a table for a counter. The clerk can stand behind the counter.
✷ You also need a chair or an armchair, where the customer sits at the end.
✷ Get an old telephone directory to be the dictionary. Make a cover for it with paper and write "Oxfurd Dictionary of English." Because it's old, you can rip off some pages and it will be funny because it's a very thick book.

At the Bookstore[1]

CHARACTERS *Clerk*
Woman

WOMAN Good morning.

CLERK Can I help you?

WOMAN Oh, yes. Do you have the book "Juliet and Romeo?"

CLERK Ah, you mean "Romeo and Juliet" by Shakespeare.

WOMAN No, no, by Chiquitita de Nava.

CLERK Ma'am, I'm sure "Romeo and Juliet" was written by William Shakespeare.

WOMAN No, no, Shakespeare wrote "Romeo and Juliet." I'm looking for "Juliet and Romeo" by the great Mexican author Chiquitita de Nava.

CLERK Well then, we don't have it.

WOMAN *(Looking around.)* That's interesting. You have a lot of books here.

CLERK *(A little disturbed.)* Yes, we do, but we don't have "Juliet and Romeo" by Chiquitita de Nada.

WOMAN De Nava!

CLERK De Nava... of course.

WOMAN That's too bad. It's much better than "Romeo and Juliet" by Shakespeare.

CLERK Better?

WOMAN Yes, the story has more details.

CLERK I'm sorry, but I don't have it.

WOMAN Oh, OK. How about "Hare?"

1. Inspired by the sketch "The Bookshop", by Monty Python.

CLERK Oh, we have that one. *(Moves towards the shelf to get it.)*

WOMAN That's "H-A-R-E," also by Chiquitita de Nava.

CLERK *(Pause.)* In that case, we don't have it. We have "Hair," H-A-I-R, the musical, but not "Hare," H-A-R-E by Chiquitita de Nada.

WOMAN De Nava!

CLERK Yes, de Nava. In fact, we don't have anything by Chiquitita de Nava. Actually, she's not very popular.

WOMAN Not very popular? She's my favorite writer.

CLERK Well, sorry.

WOMAN Do you have "The Last Good Buy?"

CLERK *(Happy.)* Yes, it's a very good book. *(Moves towards the shelf to get it.)*

WOMAN That's buy, B-U-Y.

CLERK *(Coming back.)* Definitely not. I don't have it.

WOMAN *(Moving towards door.)* Sorry to trouble you. Thanks anyway.

CLERK No problem.

WOMAN Bye.

CLERK Bye bye.

WOMAN *(Turning around.)* Excuse me!

CLERK *(Trying to control himself.)* Anything else?

WOMAN I wonder if you have "The Hunchback of Dotre Name."

CLERK No, as I told you we don't have anything by Chiquitita de Nava.

WOMAN No, not Chiquitita de Nava. Victor Huggo.

CLERK *(Happy.)* Victor Hugo?

WOMAN Yes.

CLERK *(Excitedly.)* You mean "The Hunchback of Notre Dame."

WOMAN No, "The Hunchback of Dotre Name" by Victor Huggo. That's Huggo with two gs, the famous Canadian writer.

CLERK *(After a pause.)* No, well, we don't have "The Hunchback of Dotre Name" by

Victor Huggo, the famous Canadian writer and we don't have "The Hunchback of Sotre Vame" by Hictor Vugo or "The Hunchback of Votre Same" by Mictor Pugo. Why don't you go to Barney's Bookstore?[2]

WOMAN I've been there. They sent me here.

CLERK Did they?

WOMAN Oh, I wonder if you have "The Wonderful Marvelous Fantastic Great Adventures of An Intelligent Brilliant Good Looking But A Little Tired English Teacher at Super English School",[3] volume 18.

CLERK *(After a pause.)* No, we don't have that. *(Looks around.)* Funny, we have a lot of books here. Well, I don't want to take too much of your time. *(Points to the door.)* Good bye, thank you.

WOMAN Do you have...

CLERK *(Interrupting her.)* No, we don't! No, we don't!

WOMAN But... I...

CLERK Sorry, no. *(Looking at his watch.)* Anyway, we are closing for lunch.

WOMAN Closing for lunch? But it's nine o'clock in the morning!...

CLERK In that case, we are closing for breakfast.

WOMAN But I saw the book over there.

CLERK I'm sorry...

WOMAN I saw it there. I saw it!

CLERK *(Shouts.)* What? What? What?!?

WOMAN I saw it over there. *(Points.)* "Oxfurd Dictionary of English."[4]

CLERK *(After a pause.)* "Oxfurd Dictionary of English?"

WOMAN Yes.

CLERK Oxfurd, O-X-F-U-R-D?

WOMAN Yes.

CLERK Dictionary, D-I-C-T-I-O-N-A-R-Y?

2. Use the name of a popular bookstore in your city.

3. Use the name of your school.

4. Use the name of a dictionary your students are familiar with.

WOMAN Yes.

CLERK Well, we do have that... *(Moves towards the shelf to get it.)*

WOMAN The simplified edition...

CLERK *(After a pause, politely.)* I'm sorry, I didn't understand very well.

WOMAN The simplified edition.

CLERK *(Exploding.)* The simplified edition of "Oxfurd Dictionary of English?"

WOMAN The one without the letter "C."

CLERK *(Very surprised.)* The one without the letter "C?" All Oxfurd Dictionaries of English come with the letter "C." Every dictionary comes with the letter "C."

WOMAN Well, I don't like it.

CLERK *(Furious.)* All right, I'll remove it. *(Rips some pages out of the book.)* Any other letters you don't like?

WOMAN I don't like the letter "P."

CLERK *(Screaming.)* The letter "P!" Right! The letter "P!" *(Rips some pages out of the book.)* There you are! Any others you don't like, any others?

WOMAN The letter "W."

CLERK Right! *(Flipping through the book.)* Letter "W..." Letter "W..." Letter "W..." *(Rips some pages out of the book.)* There you are! No "C"s, no "P"s, no "W"s! There's your dictionary! *(Gives it to her.)*

WOMAN I can't buy that. It's all torn! You tore the pages! *(The clerk moans.)* I wonder if you have...

CLERK Sure, ask me anything. We have lots of books here. *(Shouts.)* It's a bookstore!

WOMAN Well, how about "War and Piece?" Piece, P-I-E-C-E.

CLERK No, no, we don't have that. Strange...

WOMAN "On the Rode." Rode, R-O-D-E.

CLERK No, no, no, try again...

WOMAN "Cinderella."

CLERK No, no, no, no... *(Realizing.)* What?

WOMAN "Cinderella."

CLERK "Cinderella..." Yes, yes, yes! I have it! *(Tries to find it on the shelf.)* I've seen it somewhere. I know it! *(Laughs.)* Hee, hee, hee, hee, hee!!! Ha ha hoo hoo! Wait! Wait! *(Gets the book.)* Is that it? Is that it? Yes! Here's your book. *(Gives it to her.)* Now buy it!

WOMAN *(Quickly.)* I don't have enough money.

CLERK I'll take a deposit.

WOMAN I don't have *any* money.

CLERK I'll take a check.

WOMAN I don't have a checkbook.

CLERK *(Giving.)* Here's one. Use mine!

WOMAN I don't have a bank account!

CLERK Right! I'll buy it for you! *(Giving her the book and the money.)* There you are! There's your change! There's some money for a taxi home. There's your book. Now go!

WOMAN Wait! Wait!

CLERK What?

WOMAN I can't read.

CLERK *(After a long pause. Very quietly.)* You can't... read. *(Pause.)* Right! *(Shouts.)* Sit down! Sit down! Sit! *(She sits.)* Are you sitting comfortably? Right! *(Opens the book and reads.)* "Cinderella. Once upon a time in a faraway kingdom, there was a nice man who lived with his daughter..."

THE END

Beauty Sleep

LEVEL OF ENGLISH: Basic

RECOMMENDED AGE: Children and teenagers

STRUCTURES:

Grammar: Simple present, present continuous and future with "will" and "going to"
Vocabulary: nothing specific

NUMBER OF CHARACTERS: 2 – Sleeping Girl and Prince

COSTUMES: Get ideas from fairy tale books and movies. The costumes should be exaggerated to look funny.

PLAYING TIME: Approximately 2 minutes

SOME SUGGESTIONS:

✸ You don't need specific scenery to perform this sketch. The girl can lie on the floor.
✸ The actor who plays the Prince has to exaggerate a lot – use large gestures, speak in a very heroic and romantic way. The more he exaggerates, the funnier it will be.

Beauty Sleep

CHARACTERS *Sleeping Girl*
Prince

(The girl is sleeping. The prince enters.)

PRINCE *(To the audience.)* I'm a prince. I'm looking for a princess. There is a princess sleeping in this palace for a hundred years. I'm going to wake her up and marry her. *(Sees Sleeping Girl.)* Oh, there she is. What can I do? I know! I have my alarm clock here. *(Shows his alarm clock.)* It will ring and wake her up. *(Alarm clock rings. Sleeping Girl doesn't wake up.)* It didn't work!... I know! I'm going to imitate a rooster. *(He does. Sleeping Girl doesn't wake up.)* It didn't work!... I know! I'm going to play very loud music. *(He gets a CD player and plays very loud music. Sleeping Girl doesn't wake up.)* It didn't work! Well, I have no choice: I'm going to kiss her! *(He does.)*

SLEEPING *(Waking up.)* Who are you?

PRINCE I'm a prince. I'm looking for a princess. I woke you up and now I'm going to marry you.

SLEEPING You can't marry me! I'm married!

PRINCE Aren't you Sleeping Beauty?

SLEEPING No, I'm her neighbor. She lives next door.

PRINCE But you were sleeping so deeply!

SLEEPING Yes. I put some cotton in my ears. *(Takes the cotton from her ears and shows it.)* I was just getting my beauty sleep.

PRINCE So you're not a princess?

SLEEPING No.

PRINCE Sorry! Well, I have to go! I'm going to find Sleeping Beauty. I'm going to wake her up and marry her. *(Exits.)*

SLEEPING *(Calling.)* Prince! Prince! *(To the audience.)* Well, he's going to get a surprise! Sleeping Beauty married another prince many years ago... Didn't he watch the Disney film?

THE END

CINDERELLA

LEVEL OF ENGLISH: Basic

RECOMMENDED AGE: Any age. This sketch works well with children, teenagers and adults. Students usually like to make fun of familiar stories.

STRUCTURES:

Grammar: Simple present, present continuous and future with "going to"
Vocabulary: nothing specific

NUMBER OF CHARACTERS: 3 – Cinderella, the prince and the fairy godmother

COSTUMES: Get ideas from fairy tale books. Cinderella needs two dresses – an old one and a new one. When the fairy gives her the new dress, she can put it on over the old one.

PLAYING TIME: Approximately 5 minutes

SOME SUGGESTIONS:

- You don't need any special setting. The prince needs a chair to sit on and a newspaper.

Cinderella

CHARACTERS *Fairy*
Prince
Cindy (Cinderella)

(The three characters are on stage. Cinderella is wearing an old dress.)

FAIRY *(To the audience.)* I'm a fairy. Fairy tales are stories about magic.

PRINCE *(To the audience.)* I'm a prince. In fairy tales, there are princes and princesses.

CINDY *(To the audience.)* I'm a princess. My name is Cinderella.

FAIRY *(Looking at Cinderella's clothes.)* Cinderella, your clothes are very ugly. *(Waves her magic wand.)* Alakazoola, Mentchikaboola![1]

(Cinderella puts on her new dress, while the lights flicker.)

CINDY *(Turning around.)* Oh, thank you, Fairy Godmother.

PRINCE *(To Cinderella.)* Oh, Cinderella, you're so beautiful!

(The Fairy Godmother waves her magic wand. Cinderella and the Prince freeze.)

FAIRY Plim! Cinderella and the Prince got married. And this is what happened ***after*** the wedding. *(Waves her magic wand.)* Plim! *(Disappears.)*

(Cinderella is trying to zip up her dress. The prince sits down and reads the newspaper.)

CINDY Help me with my dress, please.

PRINCE I'm reading the newspaper.

CINDY I need help.

1. The fairy can sing the song from the movie "Cinderella."

PRINCE OK. *(Stands up and helps her to zip up her dress.)* I'm hungry.

CINDY So?

PRINCE I want to eat.

CINDY There's some pizza in the freezer.

PRINCE Again?

CINDY If you don't want pizza, go to Super Burger.[2]

PRINCE There's no Super Burger here. This is a fairy tale.

CINDY OK. OK. I'm going to call the Fairy Godmother. Maybe she can make lunch. *(Calling.)* Fairy Godmother!

FAIRY *(Appearing.)* What now?

CINDY We're hungry.

FAIRY So?

CINDY We want to eat.

FAIRY There's some pizza in the freezer.

PRINCE Oh, come on. You're a Fairy Godmother. Use your magic.

FAIRY I can't.

PRINCE Why not?

FAIRY It's Saturday. I don't work on Saturdays. Why don't you go to Super Burger?

PRINCE There's no Super Burger here. This is a fairy tale.

FAIRY Well, excuse me now. I'm going to the movies. I'm going to see Leonardo di Caprio.[3] I love Leonardo di Caprio. Oh, Leonardo... Oh, Leonardo... Oh, Leonardo... *(Exits.)*

CINDY I can't believe it!

PRINCE OK, Cindy. Let's go to the restaurant.

CINDY OK, but I need a new dress.

PRINCE Another one?

2. Use the name of a famous fast food restaurant in your area.
3. Use the name of a popular actor at the moment.

CINDY Yes, this dress is old. I'm going to call the Fairy Godmother.

PRINCE She's at the movies.

CINDY But I want a new dress. I want it! I want it! I want it! *(Calls.)* Fairy Godmother!

FAIRY *(Appearing, annoyed.)* What?

CINDY I want a new dress.

FAIRY Why?

CINDY To go to the restaurant.

FAIRY And I want to see Leonardo di Caprio. Leave me alone!

CINDY I can't go out wearing this dress. I'm a princess. Do something!

FAIRY You <u>were</u> a princess. Now you are a frog. Plim! *(Waves her magic wand. Cinderella becomes a frog, and exits, hopping.)*[4] Now let's go to the movies, Prince.

PRINCE Oh, OK. *(Exits.)*

FAIRY *(To the audience.)* Now I'm going to transform the prince into Leonardo di Caprio. *(Points to the backstage and waves her magic wand.)* Plim! Oh, Leonardo, Leonardo, Leonardo!... *(To the audience.)* I love fairy tales! *(Exits.)*

THE END

4. Since you can't transform the actress into a frog, she can just pretend she became a frog and start hopping.

Confusions

LEVEL OF ENGLISH: Basic

RECOMMENDED AGE: Teenagers and adults

STRUCTURES:

This play focuses on some confusions that English students make in English, especially pronunciation mistakes – "three" x "free" x "tree," "sheep" x "ship," "third" x "turd," "snake" x "snack," etc.

NUMBER OF CHARACTERS: 2 – An actor and an actress. You can have many more actors, who can perform the various sketches in this play. Distribute the lines accordingly.

COSTUMES: If there are only two actors, it's best to wear black clothes and add a little detail for each sketch – a hat, a shirt, a jacket, a pair of glasses, etc. These details will define the different characters in the story. If you decide to have more actors, they can create more complete costumes for the characters.

PLAYING TIME: Approximately 15 minutes

SOME SUGGESTIONS:

✷ In this play, it's important that the actors speak to the audience and encourage them to answer. However, they shouldn't force anybody to participate if the audience doesn't feel comfortable enough to.
✷ There are parts where the actors speak to the audience and parts where they perform the little sketches. A good way to separate these parts is by playing a piece of music. While the music is playing, the actors put on the clothes they're going to wear for that sketch. This can be done on stage. If the actors are wearing black clothes, they just put something on on top.
✷ For this play you will need a lot of props. Make posters with the confusing words, including the words and the pictures – birthday, bird day, burst day, three, tree, free, third, turd, feeling, filling, sheep, ship, snake, snack, two, chew, beach (with a picture of a smile), leave and live. You'll also need a suitcase, a toy snake and a basket with apples.

Confusions

CHARACTERS *Actor*
Actress

(Music. Actor and Actress enter. They talk to the audience.)

ACTOR Confusions, confusions! Life is full of confusions!

ACTRESS Confusions are confusing.

ACTOR Yeah. Confusions make us confused.

ACTRESS *(To Actor.)* This conversation is confusing, too.

ACTOR *(To Actress.)* Are you confused?

ACTRESS A little.

ACTOR Good.

ACTRESS Good?

ACTOR I'm sorry, but this is a play about confusions. It's supposed to be confusing. And you're supposed to be confused.

ACTRESS Well, I guess I am. *(Points to the audience.)* And everybody else is confused, too.

ACTOR *(To the audience.)* There are many confusing situations in our lives.

ACTRESS *(To Actor.)* You mean many situations that make us confused, right?

ACTOR Right. For example, learning a foreign language can be very confusing.

ACTRESS *(To the audience.)* Do you agree that learning a language is confusing?[1] *(The audience answers, hopefully.)*

ACTOR *(To the audience.)* Do you get confused sometimes? *(The audience answers, hopefully.)*

ACTRESS Well, we don't want to make you more confused. *(She exits.)*

1. If they don't answer, ask the question again.

ACTOR Right. We just want to show you that it's OK to be confused. If you feel confused sometimes, don't worry. You're normal. You see, English can be confusing sometimes. For example, a big confusion that sometimes happens in English has to do with the word "birthday." And the big problem is your tongue.

ACTRESS *(Pointing to her tongue.)* My tongue?

ACTOR Everybody's tongue. *(To the audience.)* Show me your tongues, please. *(They do.)*

ACTRESS *(To the audience.)* You know that for you to pronounce the "th" sounds, you have to place your tongue between your teeth and exhale, like this. *(She does it. To the audience.)* Can you do that?

ACTOR Very good, guys! Now look at these three words. *(Shows three cards, with the words "birthday," "bird day," and "burst day.")* This is "birthday." Repeat everybody, "Birthday." This is "Bird Day." It's the Day of the Birds. Repeat everybody, "Bird Day." This is "Burst Day." It's the Day of the Explosion. Repeat everybody, "Burst Day." The only way for you to pronounce "Birthday" correctly is to place your tongue between your teeth. Repeat everybody, "Birthday." *(They do it.)* Very good.

ACTRESS Yes, pronouncing the "th" sound is very important. But we have to practice it.

ACTOR And if a little saliva comes out of your mouth when you're doing it, don't worry – be happy. You're speaking English perfectly. *(He exits.)*

ACTRESS The same thing happens with the words "three", "tree" and "free." *(Shows cards with the three words.)* If you don't place your tongue between your teeth, you won't pronounce the number three correctly. Let's try it together. Repeat, "Three." *(They do it.)* Very good. One more time, "Three." *(They do it.)* Excellent. If you pronounce the number "three" correctly, you'll avoid a lot of confusion. Let's see what happens when we don't pronounce the word "three" correctly.

(Music. Actor enters.)

ACTOR Do you like dogs?

ACTRESS Yes, I do. I love dogs.

ACTOR Do you have a dog?

ACTRESS Yes. My dog is free today.[2]

ACTOR Oh, really? Did he run away?

ACTRESS No, he's at home. And today's he's free.

ACTOR Didn't you say he was at home?

2. She means "three."

ACTRESS Yes. Today is his birthday. He's free.

ACTOR Oh, I see. It's his birthday. You gave him his freedom on his birthday.

ACTRESS *(To the audience.)* Oh, nobody understands me. Why didn't I study at Super English School?[3]

(Music.)

ACTOR And now we are going to tell you a secret.

(Actor and Actress look at each other. They put their index fingers in front of their mouths.)

ACTOR & ACTRESS Shhh!

ACTOR Look at these two words. *(Shows cards with the words "third" and "turd" written.)* This is "third," the ordinal number that comes after "second." This is "turd." It means "animal excrement." So be careful with the pronunciation. Repeat everybody, "third." *(They all repeat.)* Imagine you get home and you say to your wife, "Honey, today my boss chose the best employees in the company and I was turd!" Your wife won't be very happy.[4]

ACTRESS There are many words in English whose sounds are very similar. There is a very small difference in pronunciation. You have to be careful, or you can cause a big confusion.

ACTRESS Take a look at these words. *(Shows cards with the words "feeling" and "filling.")*

ACTOR Repeat everybody, "Feeling." *(They repeat it.)* Repeat everybody, "Filling." *(They repeat it.)* A feeling is an emotion. A filling is what the dentist puts in your teeth when you have a cavity. Repeat everybody, "Feeling." *(They repeat it.)* Repeat everybody, "Filling." *(They repeat it.)*

(Music.)

ACTOR Why are you so sad?

ACTRESS You don't pay attention to my fillings.[5]

ACTOR Why should I pay attention to your fillings?

3. Use the name of your school.
4. If you're working with young students who don't work yet, you might change "wife" to "father" and say, "Daddy, today I had a competition at school, and I was turd."
5. She means "feelings."

ACTRESS My fillings are important to me. They hurt a lot.

ACTOR I'm sorry. Open your mouth.

ACTRESS What?

ACTOR *(Opens her mouth and looks inside.)* Oh, what beautiful fillings! Your dentist did a great job.

ACTRESS *(To the audience.)* Oh, nobody understands me. Why didn't I study at Super English School?[6]

(Music.)

ACTRESS *(Showing a picture of a sheep.)* What's this? *(The audience answers, hopefully.)* It's a sheep.

ACTOR *(Showing the picture of a ship.)* What's this? *(The audience answers, hopefully.)* It's a ship.

ACTRESS Repeat everybody! "Sheep." *(They repeat.)* "Ship." *(They repeat.)*

ACTOR Let's see what might happen if you don't pronounce these words correctly.

(Music.)

ACTRESS *(Carrying a suitcase.)* I'm late. I have to catch my sheep.[7]

ACTOR Are you a farmer?

ACTRESS No.

ACTOR How come you have sheep?

ACTRESS It's not my sheep. I need to catch the sheep. I'm going to Europe.

ACTOR Are you going to take the sheep to Europe?

ACTRESS No, the sheep is going to take me to Europe.

ACTOR Can the sheep swim?

ACTRESS No, but it's very big and it can float. *(Actor makes a puzzled face. To the audience.)* Oh, nobody understands me. Why didn't I study at Super English School?[8]

6. Use the name of your school.
7. She means "ship."
8. Use the name of your school.

(Music.)

ACTOR Oh, I'm so hungry.

ACTRESS You're hungry? Come to my fast food restaurant.

(Music.)

ACTRESS *(Wearing an apron.)* Can I help you?

ACTOR I'd like snake[9] number 2, please.

ACTRESS Snake number 2? Sorry, we don't serve snakes here.

ACTOR You don't? I always buy snakes here!

ACTRESS There must be some kind of mistake. This is a fast food place.

ACTOR I know. Can you give me a snake fast?

ACTRESS *(Getting a snake from under the counter.)* OK. The customer is always right. Here's your snake.

ACTOR *(Screams.)* Ahhh! Nobody understands me. Why didn't I study at Super English School?[10]

(Music.)

ACTRESS *(To the audience.)* What was the confusion in this story? *(The audience answers, hopefully.)*

ACTOR Very good! So let's practice these confusing words.

ACTRESS *(Showing a picture of a snake.)* What's this? It's a snake.

ACTOR *(Showing the picture of a snack.)* What's this? It's a snack.

ACTRESS Repeat everybody! "Snake." *(They repeat.)* "Snack." *(They repeat.)* Very good! What do you eat? Snakes or snacks?

ACTOR *(To Actress.)* There are people who eat snakes, you know.

ACTRESS *(To the audience.)* How many of you eat snakes? *(Few people answer, hopefully.)* How many of you eat snacks? *(More people answer. To Actor.)* See?

9. He means "snack."

10. Use the name of your school.

ACTOR But I'm still hungry.

ACTRESS *(Showing a basket with apples.)* Look at these apples.

ACTOR What beautiful apples!

ACTRESS Would you like some?

ACTOR Yes. Chew,[11] please.

ACTRESS OK. *(Gets an apple, bites it and chews it.)*

ACTOR What are you doing?

ACTRESS You said, "chew," right?

ACTOR Yes, "chew." *(Shows the number 2 with his fingers.)*

ACTRESS OK. For the second time. *(Chews again and shows the number 2.)*

ACTOR *(To the audience.)* Oh, nobody understands me. Why didn't I study at Super English School?[12]

(Music.)

ACTRESS Well, guys. *(Showing the cards with the words "Chew" and "Two.")* These are two tricky words. Repeat everybody, "Chew." *(They repeat.)* Repeat everybody, "Two." *(They repeat.)*

ACTOR Let's see if you got it. Let's play a game. I'm going to say a word. If I say "chew," you go like this. *(Chews.)* And if I say "two," you do this. *(Shows two fingers.)* OK, do you understand? *(They do, hopefully.)* Here we go: two, chew, chew, two, two, two, chew, two, chew, chew.

ACTRESS Very good. *(To Actor.)* Have you seen the movie "Terminal," with Tom Hanks?

ACTOR No, I haven't. Is it good?

ACTRESS It's excellent. There are so many interesting stories that happen in airports.

ACTOR That's right. *(Music. Wearing an American hat.)* Tell me about your country.

ACTRESS *(Wearing yellow and green, the colors of the Brazilian flag.)* I'm from Brazil. Brazil is very beautiful. And there are many bitches[13] in Brazil.

ACTOR *(Surprised.)* Really?

11. He means "two."
12. Use the name of your school.
13. She means "beaches."

ACTRESS Yes, of course. There are bitches in the south, bitches in the southeast, but the bitches in the northeast are the most beautiful ones. Would you like to come to Brazil with me and visit our most famous bitches?

ACTOR *(With a horny face.)* Yeah!

ACTRESS Great! My grandmother and I will go with you.

ACTOR Your... grandmother? You're taking your grandmother to visit the bitches?

ACTRESS Sure. She loves bitches.

ACTOR No way! This is too much for me. *(Exits.)*

ACTRESS My grandmother is so nice! *(To the audience.)* Oh, nobody understands me. Why didn't I study at Super English School?[14]

(Music.)

ACTOR Well, my friends, some confusions can be really serious. Do you see how important a smile is? For you to pronounce the word "beach" *(Shows card.)* you have to smile. Repeat everybody, "Beach." *(They repeat.)* If you don't smile, you're going to say a different word.

ACTRESS *(Covers his mouth.)* Don't say it!

ACTOR Here's another example, using the same sounds /I/ and /i:/.

ACTRESS This is a hospital, I'm a doctor and *(Points to Actor.)* this is my patient. And the patient is a little impatient.

(Music.)

PATIENT Doctor, am I going to live[15] today?

DOCTOR Yes, sure. You are getting better.

PATIENT Good. *(Starts packing.)*

DOCTOR *(Holding the patient.)* Where are you going?

PATIENT I'm living. *(Desperate.)* I'm living.

DOCTOR Yes, I know. You're getting better.

14. Use the name of your school.
15. He means "leave."

PATIENT I want to live! I want to live!

DOCTOR You *are* going to live. But you have to stay in the hospital a few more days.

PATIENT But if I stay in the hospital I won't live.

DOCTOR Of course you will. We'll take care of you.

PATIENT *(To the audience.)* Oh, nobody understands me. Why didn't I study at Super English School?[16]

(We hear music.)

ACTRESS Did you notice the confusion in this scene? What was it? *(They answer, hopefully.)* Very good. "To leave" means "to go, to exit," and "to live" is the opposite of "to die."

ACTOR *(To the audience.)* Well, it's time to leave.

ACTRESS Leave or live?

ACTOR Leave. Let's go. The play is over.

ACTRESS Thank you, everybody. Oh, I forgot. *(To Actor.)* Last month was your birthday and I have a present for you. *(She gets a box.)*

ACTOR A present for me?

ACTRESS Yes. Here it is. *(Gives it to him.)* Open it!

ACTOR *(Opening the box and taking a sheet out of it.)* Oh, a sheet.

ACTRESS *(To the audience.)* Thank God he knows how to pronounce this word.

ACTOR Of course! I studied at Super English School![17]

BOTH Good bye, everybody!

THE END

16. Use the name of your school.
17. Use the name of your school.

Count it Higher

LEVEL OF ENGLISH: Basic

RECOMMENDED AGE: Children, ages 6 to 12

STRUCTURES:

Grammar: Simple present
Vocabulary: Numbers from 1 to 10

NUMBER OF CHARACTERS: 11 – The announcer, 5 judges and 5 contestants. The announcer has the most difficult lines. The judges and the contestants have very simple lines.

COSTUMES: The announcer can wear fancy clothes. He or she should have a microphone. The judges can wear elegant clothes. The contestants can wear ordinary clothes.

PLAYING TIME: Between 4 and 6 minutes

SOME SUGGESTIONS:

- You don't need special scenery to present this sketch.
- The announcer should talk to the audience as if he were talking to the camera.
- Notice that the judges' last names rhyme with their numbers.
- At the end of the play, they could sing a song about numbers. The song "Count it Higher," from Sesame Street is a nice song to use here, and can be easily found on CD.

Count it Higher

CHARACTERS	*Announcer* *Jane Little, Contestant 1* *Dolly Tall, Contestant 2* *Julie Short, Contestant 3* *John Good, Contestant 4* *Sam Shy, Contestant 5* *Charlie Chun, Judge 1* *Peggy Sue, Judge 2* *Tommy Lee, Judge 3* *Susan Gore, Judge 4* *Kevin Clive, Judge 5*
ANNOUNCER	Ladies and gentleman, welcome to another edition of "Count it Higher." On our program you have to count as high as you can. Here are the judges of our competition. Here's Charlie Chun, judge number one.
CHUN	*(Enters.)* Hello.
ANNOUNCER	Peggy Sue, judge number two.
SUE	*(Enters.)* Hi, everybody.
ANNOUNCER	Tommy Lee, judge number three.
LEE	*(Enters.)* Good evening.
ANNOUNCER	Susan Gore, judge number four.
GORE	*(Enters.)* Hi, there.
ANNOUNCER	And Kevin Clive, judge number five.
CLIVE	*(Enters.)* How are you?
ANNOUNCER	And here's the first contestant, Miss Jane Little.
LITTLE	*(Enters.)* Hello.
ANNOUNCER	Welcome to our program.
LITTLE	Thank you.
ANNOUNCER	Are you ready?

LITTLE Yes, I am.

ANNOUNCER Then start counting!

LITTLE 1... 1... 1...

CHUN Sorry, time is up.

LITTLE Oh, let me try again.

CHUN Sorry, you can't.

(Chun moves to the side.)

ANNOUNCER And here's another contestant. Miss Dolly Tall.

TALL *(Enters.)* Oh, I'm so nervous.

ANNOUNCER Don't be nervous. Just relax and start counting.

TALL OK. I'll try.

ANNOUNCER Are you ready?

TALL Yes, I am.

ANNOUNCER Then start!

TALL 1, 3, 5, 7, 9...

SUE Sorry, you have to count all the numbers.

TALL Oh, I'm sorry.

(Tall moves to the side.)

ANNOUNCER Let's meet another contestant. Welcome Miss Julie Short.

SHORT *(Enters.)* Hi! Hello, Mommy! Hello, Daddy! Hello, Brother! Hello, Sister! Hello, Grandma! Hello, Grandpa...

ANNOUNCER *(Interrrupting.)* OK, OK... Are you ready to count?

SHORT Yes, I'm ready. I love to count. I always count. Counting is my life.

ANNOUNCER *(Interrupting.)* I understand. So start counting!

SHORT 10, 9, 8, 7, 6...

LEE *(Interrupting.)* Sorry. You have to start with number one.

SHORT *(Dramatic.)* Oh, tragedy! Oh, how sad!...

ANNOUNCER Good bye, Julie.

SHORT Good bye. Good bye, Mommy! Good bye, Daddy! Good bye, Brother! Good bye, Sister! Good bye, Grandma! Good bye, Grandpa...

(Short moves to the side.)

ANNOUNCER And here's our next contestant. Mr. John Good.

GOOD *(Enters.)* Hello. Give me the prize. I am the best.

ANNOUNCER Well, you have to count first.

GOOD I am the best counter in the world.

ANNOUNCER Let's see. Start!

GOOD One, dois, three, quatro, five, seis, seven, oito, nine, dez.[1]

GORE Sorry, you have to count in English.

GOOD But I can count in many languages.

GORE I'm sorry...

(Good moves to the side.)

ANNOUNCER And here's our last contestant, Mr. Sam Shy.

SHY *(Enters, very shy.)* Hello.

ANNOUNCER Excuse me, can you speak louder?

SHY *(Louder.)* Hello.

ANNOUNCER Do you like to count? *(Shy nods.)* So start counting!

SHY *(Starts softly and then gets more and more excited.)* 1, 2, 3, 4, 5, 6, 7, 8, 9, 10, 11, 12, 13, 14, 15, 16, 17, 18, 19, 20.

CLIVE Excellent! We have a winner!

1. Alternate numbers in English and in your native language.

(Everybody claps.)

ANNOUNCER *(To Shy.)* You are our champion. Congratulations!

SHY Thank you.

ANNOUNCER And that's the end of our program. Don't miss, next week, another edition of "Count it Higher!" See you there!

(Everybody waves.)

THE END

Don't Leave Me

LEVEL OF ENGLISH: Intermediate to advanced. The students have to know if-clauses.

RECOMMENDED AGE: Teenagers and adults

STRUCTURES:

Grammar: If-clauses – first, second and third conditionals
Vocabulary: Parting verbs: go away, leave, abandon

NUMBER OF CHARACTERS: 2 – John and Mary

COSTUMES: Ordinary clothes. The characters can be any age, but old enough to be married, and the clothes they wear have to reflect that. If you're working with teenagers, they can wear their parents' clothes.

PLAYING TIME: Approximately 5 minutes

SOME SUGGESTIONS:

✷ You can use chairs and a table as scenery, trying to make it look like the couple's home.
✷ You can have different pairs of students present this sketch and create a different ending. Then the class can vote for the best ending.
✷ After performing this sketch, ask the students to write a sketch using the same grammar structures. They can write a sketch about a teacher and a student, a mother and a child, etc.

Don't Leave Me

CHARACTERS *John, the husband*
Mary, the wife

(John and Mary are at home, holding hands.)

JOHN *(Romantically.)* Oh, Mary, I love you so much!

MARY *(Romantically.)* I love you, too, John.

(They kiss.)

JOHN You're the only woman for me. I can't live without you.

MARY And you're the man of my dreams. My life means nothing without you.

JOHN Oh, my love...

MARY Dear...

(They kiss passionately.)

JOHN If you left me now, you'd take away the biggest part of me.

MARY Don't worry, John. This will never happen!

JOHN I know it won't. That's why I said, "If you *left* me now, you *would take away* the biggest part of me. It's an untrue, impossible, or imagined situation.

MARY Yes, John, I know. But don't worry. I will never leave you.

JOHN I know, my dear. And I really love you.

MARY I love you, too, John.

JOHN But let's suppose you decided to leave me.

MARY What?

JOHN Yeah, just a supposition.

MARY Oh, come on, John...

JOHN If you went away, I would be desperate.

MARY *(Annoyed.)* I'm not going to go away.

JOHN If you left me, I would die.

MARY *(Angry.)* I'm not going to leave you, OK?

JOHN I said, "If you *left* me," just an unreal condition.

MARY *(To the audience.)* Oh, my, why did I marry an English teacher? *(To John.)* John, stop it! You're making me angry.

JOHN If you abandoned me, I would kill myself.

MARY *(Very angry.)* That's enough. *(She exits, gets her suitcase and comes back.)* Good bye, John.

JOHN Where are you going?

MARY I'm leaving you! I can't take it anymore.

JOHN Why? What have I done?

MARY You always think I'm going to leave you.

JOHN I'm just afraid. You know I can't live without you.

MARY Why don't you believe me when I say I won't leave you?

JOHN It was just an imaginary situation.

MARY Well, I'm tired. Good bye. *(Starts exiting.)*

JOHN *(Crying.)* No, Mary. Don't do this to me! If you leave me now, you'll take away the biggest part of me.[1]

MARY I don't care.

JOHN *(Crying even louder.)* Ooh, ooh, ooh, ooh, no, baby, please don't go!

MARY It's too late now!

JOHN And if you leave me now, you'll take away the very heart of me. Ooh, ooh, ooh, ooh, no, baby, please don't go!

MARY Oh, come on, stop crying...

1. This line and the next ones are taken from the song "If You Leave Me Now," by Chicago.

JOHN Ooh, ooh, ooh, ooh, girl, I just want you to stay!

MARY John, this is ridiculous!

JOHN A love like ours is love that's hard to find. How could we let it slip away?

MARY *(Embarrassed.)* John...

JOHN We've come too far to leave it all behind...

MARY Stop it!

JOHN How could we end it all this way? If you leave me now...

MARY *(Shouts.)* Stop! Don't say that again!

JOHN What's the matter? I said, "If you *leave* me now," because it's a real possibility. You're about to leave me, so I say, "If you *leave* me now, you *will take away* the biggest part of me." Because this is what is going to happen.

MARY I'm not leaving...

JOHN If you leave me now, I'll die.

MARY *(Louder.)* I'm not leaving...

JOHN If you go away now, my life will be over.

MARY *(Shouts.) I'm not going away!*

JOHN *(Happy.)* You're not? *(On his knees.)* Oh, thank you, my love. You know I can't live without you.

MARY Let me take my suitcase back to the bedroom. *(She exits and comes back.)*

JOHN Oh, Mary. You scared me. I thought you were going to leave me.

MARY But I didn't. I'm here...

JOHN Yes, my love. I love you...

MARY I love you, too.

(They kiss passionately.)

JOHN I was really afraid. I really thought you were going to go away.

MARY Oh, John, don't think about that. I didn't go away.

JOHN I know, but you almost did. I was terrified.

MARY I was very angry. I don't know what happened to me.

JOHN Oh, Mary, if you had left me, you would have taken away the biggest part of me.

MARY What?

JOHN If you had left me, you would have taken away the biggest part of me.

MARY John, I didn't leave you.

JOHN I know, honey. I said, "If you *had left* me." That's an imaginary condition in the past. You didn't leave me, and you didn't take away the biggest part of me, but if you *had left* me, you *would have taken away* the biggest part of me.

MARY John, don't start again. You're not talking to your students. I'm your wife.

JOHN *(Dramatic.)* If you had abandoned me, I would have died.

MARY *(Angry.)* Stop it!

JOHN If you had gone away, my life would have ended.

MARY *(Angrier and louder.)* Stop it, I said!

JOHN It's just an imaginary past condition...

MARY I've had it! That's enough. I'm up to here with your conditionals. *(She exits, gets her suitcase and comes back.)*

JOHN Where are you going?

MARY Back to my mother's house. I'm tired of you. *(To the audience.)* Why did I marry an English teacher?

JOHN What's wrong with English teachers?

MARY *(Shouts.)* What's wrong? *(Shouts louder.)* What's wrong? I'll tell you what's wrong. If I hadn't married an English teacher, I wouldn't have to listen to conditionals all day long... Good bye. *(Exits.)*

JOHN *(Cries.)* No, Mary! Don't go! Come back! I can't live without you... *(He sobs.)* Oh, Mary, why did you leave me? Living without you makes no sense to me. My life is empty. My life is sad. If you hadn't left me, you wouldn't have taken away the biggest part of me. But you did! You did! You left me and you took away the biggest part of me... *(Cries uncontrollably.)* Come back! Come back! I need you! I want you! I love you! Come back... *(He looks at the audience. Very dramatically.)* I'll think about it tomorrow. After all, tomorrow is another day.

(We hear the theme song from "Gone With the Wind." Blackout.)

THE END

Dry Bones

LEVEL OF ENGLISH: Basic

RECOMMENDED AGE: Children (ages 8 and above) and teenagers

STRUCTURES:

Grammar: Simple present, second conditional
Vocabulary: Parts of the body

NUMBER OF CHARACTERS: 6 skeletons. You can change the number of skeletons – the more the better.

COSTUMES: The actors can wear black clothes with pictures of skeletons on them.

PLAYING TIME: Between 5 and 10 minutes

SOME SUGGESTIONS:

- To set the scene you can draw pictures of tombs and skulls and place them on the walls.
- Make the sketch very dynamic and very loud. The skeletons are really angry. The more they shout, the funnier it is.
- At the end of the sketch you can use any song that mentions parts of the body. You might have to change the last lines, to link the sketch to the song.

Dry Bones

CHARACTERS *Skeletons 1 to 6*

(The scene takes place at a cemetery. All the skeletons are together, talking.)

SKELETON 1 Attention everybody! Quiet, please! Let's start the meeting!

SKELETON 2 Yeah! Let's start!

SKELETON 1 Do you know why we're here?

SKELETONS Yeah!

SKELETON 3 We're here because we, skeletons, are not treated fairly.

SKELETONS That's right! *(They all clap.)*

SKELETON 4 Nobody remembers us!

SKELETONS That's right! *(They all clap.)*

SKELETON 5 When they talk about the body, they talk about face and legs, and toes, and arms, and feet!

SKELETON 6 This is not fair!

SKELETONS No, it's not!

SKELETON 1 A person is more than just a face and legs and toes and arms and feet. How about what's inside? And what's inside?

SKELETONS Bones! Bones! Bones!

SKELETON 2 Look at your fingers, your toes, your arms and legs. There's something hard inside. *(Proud.)* It's called the bone.

SKELETONS Bones! Bones! Bones!

SKELETON 3 Yes, there are bones inside of you.

SKELETONS Bones! Bones! Bones!

SKELETON 4 There are many, many bones. That's amazing!

SKELETONS Bones! Bones! Bones!

SKELETON 5 There are bones inside your hand.

SKELETON 6 There are bones in your feet. They help you to stand.

SKELETON 1 There are bones in your elbow, bones in your knees.

SKELETON 2 There are a lot of wonderful bones!

SKELETON 3 You can't see them, but you can feel them. They are under you skin.

SKELETONS Bones! Bones! Bones!

SKELETON 4 And when you put all those bones together, you have a skeleton.

SKELETON 5 Yeah. This is one of our favorite words.

(They all clap.)

SKELETON 6 Bones are very important!

SKELETONS Bones! Bones! Bones!

SKELETON 1 If you didn't have any bones, you couldn't walk, run or swim. And you couldn't stand up and you couldn't sit down.

SKELETON 2 If you didn't have bones, you'd all fall down.

SKELETON 3 So don't forget. Bones are very important!

SKELETONS Bones! Bones! Bones!

SKELETON 4 And that's why we're going to walk around!

SKELETON 5 Yes! To show the power of the bones!

SKELETONS Bones! Bones! Bones!

SKELETON 6 We're going to fight!

SKELETONS Bones! Bones! Bones!

SKELETON 1 We're going to win!

SKELETONS Bones! Bones! Bones!

SKELETON 2 We have the power!

SKELETONS Bones! Bones! Bones!

SKELETON 3 Let's show them what we can do!

SKELETONS Bones! Bones! Bones!

SKELETON 4 Hit it, bones!

(They all sing.)

SKELETONS Ezekiel connected them dry bones[1]
Ezekiel connected them dry bones
Ezekiel connected them dry bones
Oh, hear the word of the Lord

Well, the foot bone's connected to the ankle bone
The ankle bone's connected to the leg bone
The leg bone's connected to the knee bone
The knee bone's connected to the thigh bone
The thigh bone's connected to the hip bone
The hip bone's connected to the back bone
The back bone's connected to the shoulder bone
The shoulder bone's connected to the neck bone
The neck bone's connected to the head bone
Oh hear the word of the Lord

Them bones, them bones gonna walk around
Them bones, them bones gonna walk around
Them bones, them bones gonna walk around
Oh hear the word of the Lord
Well, the head bone's connected to neck the bone
The neck bone's connected to the shoulder bone
The shoulder bone's connected to the back bone
The back bone's connected to the hip bone
The hip bone's connected to the thigh bone
The thigh bone's connected to the knee bone
The knee bone's connected to the leg bone
The leg bone's connected to the ankle bone
The ankle bone's connected to the foot bone
Oh, hear the word of the Lord

Oh, hear the word of the Lord

THE END

1. This is a very popular folk song.

FASHION

LEVEL OF ENGLISH: Basic

RECOMMENDED AGE: Children (ages 8 and above) and teenagers

STRUCTURES:

Grammar: Simple present, singular and plural nouns
Vocabulary: Clothing items

NUMBER OF CHARACTERS: 5 – 3 designers and 2 millionaires. You can add more characters if you are working with bigger groups. You can have 2 designers only, and more millionaires.

COSTUMES: The designers can wear ordinary clothes, and the millionaires can wear very extravagant clothes (funny hats, glasses, scarves, etc).

PLAYING TIME: Approximately 5 minutes

SOME SUGGESTIONS:

- The lines in this sketch are very simple, but if you're working with a group of students who can speak more, you can elaborate a little bit more on them.
- The designers show pictures of clothes to the millionaires to simplify the production. However, you can also use real clothes to make the sketch more interesting.
- You can end the play with a song about fashion or a song about clothes.

Fashion

CHARACTERS *Millionaires 1 and 2*
Designers 1 to 3

DESIGNER 1 Hurry up!

DESIGNER 2 I'm getting ready!

DESIGNER 3 What time is it?

DESIGNER 1 It's three-thirty.

DESIGNER 2 Oh, my God!

DESIGNER 3 Hurry up! Hurry up!

DESIGNER 1 The millionaires are coming.

DESIGNER 2 We're late!

DESIGNER 3 We're very, very late!

DESIGNER 1 Where are the pictures?

DESIGNER 2 *(Showing.)* They're here.

DESIGNER 3 I hope they like our clothes.

DESIGNER 1 *(Pointing.)* Look! Here they come!

(The millionaires enter.)

MILLIONAIRE 1 Good afternoon!

DESIGNER 2 Good afternoon!

MILLIONAIRE 2 We want to see beautiful clothes!

DESIGNER 3 Yes, of course!

MILLIONAIRE 1 Money is not important.

MILLIONAIRE 2 We're millionaires!

MILLIONAIRE 1 We won the Mega Sena![1]

MILLIONAIRE 2 We are very very rich!

DESIGNER 1 Sure.

DESIGNER 2 What are you looking for?

MILLIONAIRE 1 The latest fashion!

MILLIONAIRE 2 We're millionaires!

MILLIONAIRE 1 We have to be elegant!

MILLIONAIRE 2 Very very elegant!

DESIGNER 3 Right! Let's start the fashion show!

DESIGNER 1 *(Showing a picture.)* Look at this dress! It's beautiful!

MILLIONAIRE 1 It's too simple! I'm a millionaire.

DESIGNER 2 *(Showing a picture.)* Look at these pants. They're very chic.

MILLIONAIRE 2 They're chic for you! Not for millionaires like us!

MILLIONAIRE 1 We are very very rich!

DESIGNER 3 *(Showing a picture.)* Do you like these shoes? They're elegant!

MILLIONAIRE 2 They're ugly!

MILLIONAIRE 1 We want beautiful things.

MILLIONAIRE 2 We're millionaires!

MILLIONAIRE 1 We're very very rich!

DESIGNER 1 I understand that!

DESIGNER 2 *(Showing a picture.)* Look at this marvelous sweater!

MILLIONAIRE 2 Marvelous? It's terrible.

MILLIONAIRE 1 Look. We're...

DESIGNER 3 *(Interrupting.)* Millionaires! You're very very rich! I know!

1. The Mega Sena is a famous lottery in Brazil. Use the name of a famous lottery in your country.

MILLIONAIRE 2 That's right.

MILLIONAIRE 1 Show us the fashion!

DESIGNER 1 *(Showing a picture.)* How about this T-shirt?

DESIGNER 2 *(Showing a picture.)* This skirt?

DESIGNER 3 *(Showing a picture.)* These shorts?

DESIGNER 1 *(Showing a picture.)* These socks?

MILLIONAIRE 2 Stop!

MILLIONAIRE 1 That's enough!

MILLIONAIRE 2 Your clothes are awful!

MILLIONAIRE 1 You are offending us!

MILLIONAIRE 2 We're millionaires!

MILLIONAIRE 1 We are...

DESIGNER 2 *(Interrupting.)* Very very rich! I know!

MILLIONAIRE 2 Let's get out of here!

MILLIONAIRE 1 Yes. Let's go to "Saslú."[2]

DESIGNER 3 Wait! Don't go!

MILLIONAIRE 2 Why not?

DESIGNER 1 Before you go, let us copy your clothes!

DESIGNER 2 They're very elegant and chic.

MILLIONAIRE 1 Do you think so?

DESIGNER 3 Of course!

DESIGNER 1 We can use them to start a new collection!

MILLIONAIRE 2 Hey, I'm starting to like this place!

MILLIONAIRE 1 Yes, me too.

MILLIONAIRE 2 They know a lot about fashion!

2. Use the name of a very fashionable store in your city.

DESIGNER 2 *(To the other designers.)* Well, we know a lot about psychology!

DESIGNER 3 That's right!

(They all laugh.)

THE END

Going to the Zoo

LEVEL OF ENGLISH: Basic

RECOMMENDED AGE: Children, ages 7 and above

STRUCTURES:

Grammar: Simple present
Vocabulary: Names of animals, adjectives that describe animals and things people take to the zoo

NUMBER OF CHARACTERS: 11 – A teacher and 10 students. You can have more or fewer students, depending on the number of actors you want to use.

COSTUMES: Ordinary clothes for the students. You can have all the students wear the same colors if you want them to look like they're wearing uniforms. The teacher can wear fancy clothes, and a pair of funny glasses.

PLAYING TIME: Approximately 5 minutes

SOME SUGGESTIONS:

- Arrange the desks for the students in a semi-circle, facing the audience. The teacher stands at one of the sides, so the audience can see him/her. You can also have the students sit on the floor.
- You can add more animals to the lines of the sketch.
- The imitations of animals should be very exaggerated to be funny.
- You can end the sketch with a song about animals, for example, "Going to the Zoo."
- In English students don't address the teacher by the word "teacher." They use his or her first name or last name (John or Mr. Brown). Call students' attention to that.

Going to the Zoo

CHARACTERS *Teacher*
Students 1 to 10

(The students are together. The teacher arrives.)

TEACHER Hello, everybody!

STUDENTS Hello.

TEACHER How are you?

STUDENTS Fine, thank you.

STUDENT 1 And you?

TEACHER I'm fine, thank you. Let's start the English class.

STUDENT 2 Good. I love English!

STUDENT 3 Me too. English is fun!

TEACHER Sit down, please. *(The students sit down.)* Today we're going to the zoo.

STUDENTS Yeah! *(They all stand up and run to the door.)*

TEACHER Stop! Sit down! We're going to the zoo in our imagination.

STUDENTS *(Disappointed.)* Oh! *(They all sit down.)*

STUDENT 4 I want to go to the zoo.

STUDENT 5 I like animals.

STUDENT 6 Zoo animals are beautiful.

TEACHER *(Shows the picture of a tiger.)* What's this?

STUDENT 7 It's a tiger.

STUDENT 8 It's big!

TEACHER Who can imitate a tiger?

STUDENT 9 *(Standing up.)* I can! *(Imitates a tiger. The other students laugh.)*

STUDENT 10 I don't like tigers. I like lions. *(Imitates a lion. The other students laugh.)*

TEACHER *(Shows the picture of a lion.)* Look at this lion.

STUDENT 1 It's beautiful. And it's big.

TEACHER *(Shows picture of a giraffe.)* What's this?

STUDENT 2 I don't know.

STUDENT 3 *(Raises his hand.)* It's a giraffe.

STUDENT 4 It's tall.

TEACHER What color is the giraffe?

STUDENT 5 It's yellow and brown.

TEACHER Try to walk like a giraffe. *(All students stand up and walk like giraffes, stretching their necks.)* You're very good students.

STUDENTS Yes, we are! *(They all laugh.)*

STUDENT 6 You are a good teacher!

TEACHER Thank you. *(Shows the picture of a monkey.)* Look at this animal!

STUDENT 7 What a big tail!

STUDENT 8 Is it a monkey?

STUDENTS Yes, it is.

STUDENT 9 I can imitate a monkey! Look! *(Imitates a monkey. The other students laugh.)*

TEACHER What other zoo animals do you know?

STUDENT 10 Zebras! *(Runs around the room like a zebra.)*

STUDENT 1 Kangaroos! *(Hops like a kangaroo.)*

STUDENT 2 Bears! *(Makes the sound of a bear.)*

STUDENT 3 Hippos! *(Opens his mouth like a hippo.)*

STUDENT 4 Elephants! *(Stretches his arm in front of his nose to pretend it's an elephant's trunk and makes the sound of an elephant.)*

STUDENT 5 I like elephants! They're funny!

STUDENT 6 Yes, and they're very big.

TEACHER OK! Let's imagine we're going to the zoo. What can we take?

STUDENT 7 Let's take our cameras!

STUDENT 8 Let's take sandwiches!

STUDENT 9 Let's take popcorn!

STUDENT 10 Yeah! I like popcorn.

STUDENT 1 Let's take ice cream!

STUDENT 2 Good idea!

(All the students start talking at the same time.)

TEACHER OK! Silence, please! And now I have a surprise for you!

STUDENT 3 What is it?

TEACHER *(Gets some tickets and shows them.)* Look at these.

STUDENT 4 What are they?

STUDENT 5 Tickets!

STUDENTS Tickets?

TEACHER Yes. Tickets to go to the zoo. Let's go! The bus is outside!

STUDENT 6 Great! We're going to the zoo!

TEACHER I told you!

(They all run out.)

THE END

Little Red Riding Hood

LEVEL OF ENGLISH: Basic

RECOMMENDED AGE: Any age. Since the sketch makes fun of the original fairy tale, children, teenagers and adults will enjoy it.

STRUCTURES:

Grammar: Simple present, present continuous, "going to" future
Vocabulary: Parts of the body, sense verbs

NUMBER OF CHARACTERS: 3 – Little Red, Wolf and Grandma

COSTUMES: Little Red Riding Hood can wear a dress and a red cape with a red hood. The wolf can wear a nightgown with a tail sticking out at the bottom, and a nightcap. Grandma can wear very fashionable clothes, since she's coming back from the shopping mall.

PLAYING TIME: Approximately 5 minutes

SOME SUGGESTIONS:

- The Wolf can be sitting on a chair, covered with a sheet.
- The door can be imaginary. When the wolf knocks on it, someone can say, "Knock, knock," or you can play a recording with the sound.
- The objects in Grandma's bag should be very funny-looking.

Little Red Riding Hood

CHARACTERS	*Little Red* *Wolf* *Grandma*

(Little Red enters. She's carrying a basket.)

LITTLE RED *(To the audience.)* I'm Little Red Riding Hood. I'm going to my grandmother's house. I'm going to give her some candy. *(Sings and starts walking.)* La, la, la, la, la...

(Little Red gets to Grandma's house and knocks. The wolf is lying in bed.)[1]

WOLF *(Imitating Grandma's voice.)* Who's there?

LITTLE RED Little Red Riding Hood, Grandma.

WOLF Come in.

LITTLE RED *(Entering.)* Hello, Grandma.

WOLF Oh, hello, Little Red.

LITTLE RED I have some candy for you.

WOLF Oh, I love candy. Thank you.

(Little Red looks at the wolf. She notices something is wrong.)

LITTLE RED Grandma, you have big eyes.[2]

WOLF To see you better.[3]

LITTLE RED Grandma, you have big ears.

1. If you're working with lights, turn on the lights on the wolf at this moment. Otherwise, the wolf can enter while Little Red is walking.
2. You can use the original line, "What big eyes you have," or this simplified version.
3. You can use the original line, "The better to see you with," or this simplified version.

WOLF To hear you better.

LITTLE RED Grandma, you have big hands.

WOLF To hug you better.

LITTLE RED Grandma, you have a big nose.

WOLF To smell you better.

LITTLE RED Grandma, you have a big, wet mouth.

WOLF To eat you better. *(Stands up.)*

LITTLE RED Oh, no, help me!

(They run in circles.)

WOLF I'm going to eat you!

LITTLE RED *(Shouts.)* No! No! Help! Help! Somebody!

(Grandma enters, coming from the shopping center. She's carrying some shopping bags.)

GRANDMA What's going on here?

LITTLE RED Grandma, help me!

GRANDMA What's the matter?

LITTLE RED Can't you see? There's a wolf after me!

GRANDMA Are you playing?

LITTLE RED No!

GRANDMA What are you doing?

LITTLE RED He wants to eat me!!!!

GRANDMA *(Opening her bags.)* Wait! I just bought a pair of shoes at the shopping center.

(Little Red and the wolf continue running in circles.)

LITTLE RED Help! Help!

GRANDMA *(Getting objects from her bags and showing them.)* Wait! This is my new blouse. This is my new hat. This is my new coat. This is my new bikini. *(Finds her shoes.)* Ah, here are my shoes. *(Shouts.)* Stop! *(They stop. She hits the wolf with one of the shoes.)* Take that, you Big Bad Wolf.

WOLF Ugh! *(Falls down.)*

GRANDMA *(Still attacking him.)* And that! And that!

LITTLE RED Grandma! *(Grandma does some karate gestures. Little Red tries to hold her.)* Poor Mr. Wolf. Grandma, stop that!

(Grandma stops.)

WOLF *(Waking up, very dizzy.)* Who am I? Where am I? What am I?

LITTLE RED *(Getting near him.)* Oh, are you OK?

WOLF Who are you?

LITTLE RED I'm Little Red Riding Hood.

WOLF *(In love.)* Little Red Riding Hood. What a beautiful name!

LITTLE RED Thank you.

WOLF *(In love.)* Oh, you're so beautiful!

LITTLE RED Oh, thank you, Mr. Wolf. You're cute, too.

WOLF Do you want to marry me?

LITTLE RED Sure. Why not?

GRANDMA Oh, this is really romantic. It looks like a fairy tale. *(We hear the wedding march. Little Red and the wolf walk slowly and exit. To the audience.)* And they lived happily ever after.

THE END

Love Class

LEVEL OF ENGLISH: Basic

RECOMMENDED AGE: Children ages 7 and above

STRUCTURES:

Grammar: Simple present
Vocabulary: Words related to love and to the number two

NUMBER OF CHARACTERS: 11 – A teacher, 5 boys and 5 girls. You can add or eliminate students. Redistribute or add lines.

COSTUMES: The teacher can wear clothes that make him/her look older. Children can borrow clothes from their parents or grandparents. The students can wear a uniform; for example, blue shorts or skirt and a white T-shirt.

PLAYING TIME: Approximately 5 minutes

SOME SUGGESTIONS:

✷ You can have a classroom setting, with chairs and desks, or you can have students sit on the floor. The teacher can stand in the center.
✷ In English students don't address the teacher by the word "teacher." They use his or her first name or last name (John or Mr. Brown). Call students' attention to that.
✷ You can play a song about love at the end and have everybody sing and dance.

Love Class

CHARACTERS *Teacher*
Boys 1 to 5
Girls 1 to 5

(The students are waiting. The teacher arrives.)

TEACHER Good afternoon, class.

STUDENTS Good afternoon.

TEACHER Welcome to my Love Class. The class that will teach you everything you need to know about love.

(The girls sigh.)

GIRL 1 Love is so beautiful.

GIRL 2 Love is so romantic!

GIRL 3 It's wonderful to be in love!

(The girls sigh.)

TEACHER That's right. Love is wonderful. But there are many things you have to know about love.

BOY 1 What's the first one?

BOY 2 Tell us, please. We want to fall in love!

TEACHER Well, the most important rule is – It takes two.

STUDENTS It takes two?

TEACHER Yes, it takes two.

BOY 3 What do you mean?

TEACHER Well, you can't love alone. You need somebody else.

GIRL 4 That's very interesting. Can you give us an example?

TEACHER An example? Yes. *(Thinks.)* You're alone, so you're one. When you're with somebody that you love, you're two. One and one make two.

GIRL 5 Is this a love class or a math class?

BOY 4 I don't want to study math.

TEACHER Love and math are related. It's not good to be alone. It's much nicer to be with someone. One and one make two.

BOY 5 I'm not a good math student. Can I be a good love student?

TEACHER Of course! Everybody can learn how to love. Now let's see if you're ready for love.

GIRL 1 I'm ready for love. *(Sighs.)*

GIRL 2 Me, too. *(Sighs.)*

GIRL 3 Me, three. *(Sighs.)*

(The others laugh.)

TEACHER Why is two better than one?

BOY 1 It's not good to be alone.

BOY 2 It's more fun to be with someone.

BOY 3 Everybody needs somebody.

GIRL 4 Everybody needs to be in love.

(The girls sigh.)

TEACHER You're very good students.

BOY 4 Thank you.

BOY 5 You're a very good teacher.

TEACHER Thanks.

GIRL 5 You know, I think I am in love...

TEACHER Really?

GIRL 5 Yes. I'm in love with the number two... *(Sighs.)*

(The girls sigh again.)

THE END

Mr. Ache – Version 1

LEVEL OF ENGLISH: Basic and Intermediate

RECOMMENDED AGE: Teenagers and adults. The text can be simplified to be used by children

STRUCTURES:

Grammar: I have.../He has... to describe ailments
Vocabulary: Diseases and ailments

NUMBER OF CHARACTERS: 3 – Mr. Ache, Mrs. Young and the receptionist. See Version 2 and Version 3 for ideas of variations.

COSTUMES: Ordinary clothes. The receptionist can wear white clothes and Mr. Ache can have a scarf around his neck.

PLAYING TIME: Approximately 6 minutes

SOME SUGGESTIONS:

- You can use three chairs and a desk to set the scenery for the waiting room.
- On the receptionist's desk you can have a telephone and an appointment book.
- You can have a glass of water on the desk. This is the water that Mr. Ache will drink.

Mr. Ache – Version 1

CHARACTERS	*Receptionist* *Mrs. Young, a patient* *Mr. Ache, a hypochondriac*

(The receptionist is at her desk. Mrs. Young enters.)

YOUNG	Hi. I have an appointment with Dr. Brown.
RECEPTIONIST	Oh, Mrs. Young. Dr. Brown will see you in a few minutes. Do sit down.
YOUNG	OK. Thanks. *(Sits.)*
MR. ACHE	*(Enters running.)* Help! Help! This is an emergency!
RECEPTIONIST	Oh, Mr. Ache. You again? What's the problem this time?
MR. ACHE	Oh, I'm very, very, very sick.
RECEPTIONIST	You don't look very sick.
MR. ACHE	But I am, I am...
RECEPTIONIST	OK. Do you have an appointment?
MR. ACHE	No, this is an emergency.
RECEPTIONIST	Then please sit down and wait.
MR. ACHE	How long do I have to wait? I'm dying...
RECEPTIONIST	Don't worry, Mr. Ache. Not very long. *(To Mrs. Young.)* So, are you feeling better, Mrs. Young?
YOUNG	A little, but last week I had a terrible headache.
MR. ACHE	*(To himself.)* Oh, I have a terrible headache.
YOUNG	I took some aspirin...
MR. ACHE	*(Getting some aspirin.)* Some aspirin. *(He takes a lot of aspirin.)*
YOUNG	...but I didn't get better. I got worse!

MR. ACHE Oh, I think I'm getting worse.

RECEPTIONIST Really?

YOUNG Yes, the aspirin gave me a stomachache.

MR. ACHE Oh, I have a stomachache. *(To the receptionist.)* Please I have to see the doctor now.

RECEPTIONIST Be patient. Just wait a few more minutes.

YOUNG *(To the receptionist.)* Is he OK?

RECEPTIONIST Don't worry. He's just our local hypochondriac.

YOUNG Hypochondriac?

RECEPTIONIST Yes. He thinks he's sick all the time. He comes here very often.

YOUNG Ah, I see...

RECEPTIONIST So, you had a stomachache. *(Mr. Ache puts his hand on his stomach, as if he were feeling pain.)*

YOUNG Yeah. And I drank a lot of milk.

MR. ACHE Milk! Milk! I need some milk! Quick! Do you have any milk?

RECEPTIONIST I'm sorry, Mr. Ache, but we don't have any milk. Have some water, instead. *(Mr. Ache drinks some water.)* Did you get better after you drank milk?

YOUNG Yes, I sure did.

MR. ACHE Are you sure you don't have any milk?

YOUNG *(To Mr. Ache.)* I'm sure water is fine, too... *(Mr. Ache drinks more water. To the receptionist.)* Oh, I almost forgot. I have to make an appointment for my sister.

RECEPTIONIST Yes? What's the matter with her?

YOUNG She has an earache.

MR. ACHE *(Putting his hand on his ear.)* Oh, I have an earache! *(To the receptionist.)* This is taking too long. Can I see the doctor now?

RECEPTIONIST Calm down, Mr. Ache. *(Opening her appointment book, to Mrs. Young.)* Is Tuesday at 4 o'clock all right?

YOUNG OK.

RECEPTIONIST *(To Mrs. Young.)* By the way, how's your mother?

YOUNG Not very well. She can't walk, she can't swim, she can't dance. She can't do anything anymore.

MR. ACHE *(Well, but anxious.)* What's wrong with her? What's wrong with her?

YOUNG She has a terrible backache.

MR. ACHE *(Putting his hand on his back.)* Oh! My back hurts! I can't move!

YOUNG Sometimes it's difficult for her to breathe.

MR. ACHE *(Breathing with difficulty.)* I can't breathe! Help! Help!

RECEPTIONIST I'm so sorry to hear that. In fact, everybody in this city seems to be sick nowadays. This has been a very busy week, you know. Lots of people have the flu...

(Mr. Ache sneezes.)

YOUNG Bless you!

RECEPTIONIST My husband has a sore throat...

MR. ACHE *(Putting his hand on his throat.)* I have a sore throat!

YOUNG Yeah... And my neighbor has a fever... *(Mr. Ache puts his hand on his forehead, to see if he has a fever.)* My cousin has a cough... *(Mr. Ache coughs.)* And my poor friend Gloria broke an arm. *(Mr. Ache examines his arms desperately.)*

RECEPTIONIST And you won't believe this. My English teacher had a heart attack in the classroom.

MR. ACHE *(Putting his hand on his chest.)* Aaah! I'm having a heart attack! Quick! Do something! Aaah!

RECEPTIONIST *(Has an idea, stands up and gets some cotton from her drawer.)* I think I found the solution to your problem! Here! *(Shows him the cotton.)*

MR. ACHE What is this?

RECEPTIONIST Cotton! Put it in your ears!

MR. ACHE What?

RECEPTIONIST Just put the cotton in your ears.

MR. ACHE *(Not understanding.)* Oh, OK. *(Gets the cotton and puts it in his ears.)*

YOUNG What are you doing?

RECEPTIONIST Just watch. *(To Mr. Ache. He doesn't react, because he can't hear anything.)* Earache... Backache...Stomachache... Cough... Flu... Sore throat... Heart attack... *(Takes the cotton from his ears.)* Mr. Ache, you're cured.

MR. ACHE *(Surprised.)* I am?

RECEPTIONIST Yes, you are. You can go home now. Just remember to keep the cotton in your ears.

MR. ACHE I'm cured?

RECEPTIONIST Yes.

MR. ACHE Thank you! *(Happy, goes out, shouting.)* I'm cured! I'm cured! I'm cured! *(Exits.)*

RECEPTIONIST *(To the door.)* Bye, bye, Mr. Ache. See you next week.

THE END

Mr. Ache – Version 2

LEVEL OF ENGLISH: Basic and Intermediate

RECOMMENDED AGE: Teenagers and adults. The text can be simplified to be used for children

STRUCTURES:

Grammar: I have.../He has... to describe ailments
Vocabulary: Diseases and ailments

NUMBER OF CHARACTERS: 4 – Mr. Ache, Mrs. Young, Mrs. Smith and the receptionist. See Version 1 and Version 3 for ideas of variations.

COSTUMES: Ordinary clothes. The receptionist can wear white clothes and Mr. Ache can have a scarf around his neck.

PLAYING TIME: Approximately 6 minutes

SOME SUGGESTIONS:

- You can use four chairs and a desk to set the scenery for the waiting room.
- On the receptionist's desk you can have a telephone and an appointment book.
- You can have a glass of water on the desk. This is the water that Mr. Ache will drink.

Mr. Ache – Version 2

CHARACTERS	*Receptionist* *Mrs. Young, a patient* *Mrs. Smith, a patient* *Mr. Ache, a hypochondriac*

(A waiting room. The receptionist is at her desk. Mrs. Smith is waiting. Mrs. Young enters.)

YOUNG Hi. I have an appointment with Dr. Brown.

RECEPTIONIST Oh, Mrs. Young. Do sit down. Dr. Brown is busy with another patient. Then she'll see Mrs. Smith, and you're next.

YOUNG OK. Thanks. *(Sits. To Mrs. Smith.)* Good afternoon.

SMITH Good afternoon.

MR. ACHE *(Enters running.)* Help! Help! This is an emergency!

RECEPTIONIST Oh, Mr. Ache. You again? What's the problem this time?

MR. ACHE Oh, I'm very, very, very sick.

RECEPTIONIST You don't look very sick.

MR. ACHE But I am, I am...

RECEPTIONIST OK. Do you have an appointment?

MR. ACHE No, this is an emergency.

RECEPTIONIST Then please sit down and wait.

MR. ACHE How long do I have to wait? I'm dying...

RECEPTIONIST Don't worry, Mr. Ache. Not very long. *(To Mrs. Young.)* So, are you feeling better, Mrs. Young?

YOUNG A little, but last week I had a terrible headache.

MR. ACHE *(Putting his hand on his head, to himself.)* Oh, I have a terrible headache.

YOUNG I took some aspirin...

MR. ACHE *(Gets some aspirin.)* Some aspirin. *(He takes a lot of aspirin.)*

YOUNG ...but I didn't get better. I got worse!

MR. ACHE Oh, I think I'm getting worse.

RECEPTIONIST Really?

SMITH You got worse after you took the aspirin?

YOUNG Yes, the aspirin gave me a stomachache.

MR. ACHE *(Putting his hand on his stomach.)* Oh, I have a stomachache. *(To the receptionist.)* Please I have to see the doctor now.

RECEPTIONIST Be patient. Just wait a few more minutes.

SMITH *(To the receptionist.)* Is he OK?

RECEPTIONIST Don't worry. He's just our local hypochondriac.

SMITH Hypochondriac?

RECEPTIONIST Yes. He thinks he's sick all the time. He comes here very often.

SMITH Ah, I see... *(To Mrs. Young)* So, you had a stomachache. *(Mr. Ache puts his hand on his stomach, as if he were feeling pain.)*

YOUNG Yeah. And I drank a lot of milk.

SMITH I see.

MR. ACHE Milk! Milk! I need some milk! Quick! Do you have any milk?

RECEPTIONIST I'm sorry, Mr. Ache, but we don't have any milk. Have some water, instead. *(Mr. Ache drinks some water.)*

SMITH Did you get better after you drank milk?

YOUNG Yes, I sure did.

MR. ACHE Are you sure you don't have any milk?

SMITH *(To Mr. Ache.)* I'm sure water is fine, too... *(Mr. Ache drinks more water. To the receptionist)* Oh, I almost forgot. I have to make an appointment for my sister.

RECEPTIONIST Yes? What's the matter with her?

SMITH She has an earache.

MR. ACHE *(Putting his hand on his ear.)* Oh, I have an earache! *(To the receptionist)* This is taking too long. Can I see the doctor now?

RECEPTIONIST Calm down, Mr. Ache. *(Opening her appointment book, to Mrs. Smith.)* Is Tuesday at 4 o'clock all right?

SMITH OK.

RECEPTIONIST *(To Mrs. Smith.)* By the way, how's your mother, Mrs. Smith?

SMITH Not very well. She can't walk, she can't swim, she can't dance. She can't do anything anymore.

MR. ACHE *(Well, but anxious.)* What's wrong with her? What's wrong with her?

SMITH She has a terrible backache.

MR. ACHE *(Putting his hands on his back.)* Oh! My back hurts! I can't move!

SMITH Sometimes it's difficult for her to breathe.

MR. ACHE *(Breathing with difficulty.)* I can't breathe! Help! Help!

RECEPTIONIST I'm so sorry to hear that.

YOUNG In fact, everybody in this city seems to be sick nowadays.

RECEPTIONIST That's right. This has been a very busy week, you know. Lots of people have the flu...

(Mr. Ache sneezes.)

YOUNG Bless you!

RECEPTIONIST My husband has a sore throat...

MR. ACHE *(Putting his hand on his throat.)* I have a sore throat!

SMITH My neighbor has a fever... *(Mr. Ache puts his hand on his forehead, to see if he has a fever.)*

RECEPTIONIST My cousin has a cough. *(Mr. Ache coughs.)*

YOUNG And my poor friend Gloria broke an arm. *(Mr. Ache examines his arms desperately.)*

RECEPTIONIST And you won't believe this. My English teacher had a heart attack in the classroom.

MR. ACHE *(Putting his hand on his chest.)* Aaah! I'm having a heart attack! Quick! Do something! Aaah!

RECEPTIONIST *(Has an idea, stands up and gets some cotton from her drawer.)* I think I found the solution to your problem! Here! *(Shows him the cotton.)*

MR. ACHE What is this?

RECEPTIONIST Cotton! Put it in your ears!

MR. ACHE What?

RECEPTIONIST Just put the cotton in your ears.

MR. ACHE *(Not understanding.)* Oh, OK. *(Gets the cotton and puts it in his ears.)*

YOUNG What are you doing?

RECEPTIONIST Just watch. *(To Mr. Ache. Mr. Ache doesn't react because he can't hear.)* Stomachache... Headache... Backache... Earache... Heart attack... Stuffy nose... Cough... *(Removes the cotton.)* Mr. Ache, you're cured.

MR. ACHE *(Surprised.)* I am?

RECEPTIONIST Yes, you are. You can go home now. Just remember to keep the cotton in your ears.

MR. ACHE I'm cured?

RECEPTIONIST Yes.

MR. ACHE Thank you! *(Happy, goes out, shouting.)* I'm cured! I'm cured! I'm cured! *(Exits.)*

RECEPTIONIST *(To the door.)* Bye, bye, Mr. Ache. See you next week.

THE END

Mr. Ache – Version 3

LEVEL OF ENGLISH: Basic and Intermediate

RECOMMENDED AGE: Teenagers and adults. The text can be simplified to be used for children

STRUCTURES:

Grammar: I have.../He has... to describe ailments
Vocabulary: Diseases and ailments

NUMBER OF CHARACTERS: 2 – Mr. Ache and the receptionist. See Version 1 and Version 2 for ideas of variations.

COSTUMES: Ordinary clothes. The receptionist can wear white clothes and Mr. Ache can have a scarf around his neck.

PLAYING TIME: Approximately 6 minutes

SOME SUGGESTIONS:

- You can use two chairs and a desk to set the scenery for the waiting room.
- On the receptionist's desk you can have a telephone and an appointment book.
- You can have a glass of water on the desk. This is the water that Mr. Ache will drink.

Mr. Ache – Version 3

CHARACTERS *Receptionist*
Mr. Ache, a hypochondriac

(A waiting room. The receptionist is at her desk. The phone rings. The receptionist answers it.)

RECEPTIONIST Dr. Brown's office. Can I help you?... Yes... Yes, Mr. Green. *(Opens her appointment book.)* Is Tuesday at 4 pm OK?... OK. See you on Tuesday. *(Hangs up.)*

MR. ACHE *(Enters, running.)* Help me! Help me! This is an emergency!

RECEPTIONIST Mr. Ache? You again? What's the problem this time?

MR. ACHE I'm very, very sick.

RECEPTIONIST You don't look very sick.

MR. ACHE But I am, I am.

RECEPTIONIST OK. Do you have an appointment?

MR. ACHE No, but this is an emergency!

RECEPTIONIST OK. Then, please sit down and wait.

MR. ACHE How long do I have to wait? I'm dying.

RECEPTIONIST Don't worry, Mr. Ache. Not very long. *(The phone rings. The receptionist answers it.)* Dr. Brown's office. Can I help you?... Oh, hi, Mom. How are you?... What? You had a terrible headache yesterday?

MR. ACHE *(Putting his hand on his head, to himself.)* Oh, I have a terrible headache.

RECEPTIONIST *(On the phone.)* Did you take aspirin?

MR. ACHE *(Getting some aspirin.)* Some aspirin. *(He takes a lot of aspirin.)*

RECEPTIONIST *(On the phone.)* Oh, really? You took some aspirin but you didn't get better. You got worse.

MR. ACHE Oh, I think I'm getting worse.

RECEPTIONIST *(On the phone.)* I see, the aspirin gave you a stomachache.

MR. ACHE *(Putting his hand on his stomach, as if he has a stomachache.)* Oh, I have a terrible stomachache. *(To the receptionist.)* Please I have to see the doctor now.

RECEPTIONIST *(On the phone.)* Hold on. *(To Mr. Ache.)* Be patient, Mr. Ache. Just a few more minutes. *(Back on the phone.)* Sorry, Mom... No, it's OK. It's just our local hypochondriac... Yes, hypochondriac. He thinks he's sick all the time. He comes here very often. So you were saying you had a stomachache. *(Mr. Ache puts his hand on his stomach, as if he were feeling pain.)* Did you drink milk?

MR. ACHE Milk! Milk! I need some milk. Quick! Do you have any milk?

RECEPTIONIST *(To Mr. Ache.)* Sorry, Mr. Ache. We don't have any milk. Have some water, instead. *(Mr. Ache drinks water. On the phone)* Sorry. Oh, I see. You drank milk and felt better.

MR. ACHE Are you sure you don't have any milk?

RECEPTIONIST *(To Mr. Ache.)* Mr. Ache, I'm sure water will be fine. *(He drinks more water. On the phone.)* And how's Grandma?... Really? She has an earache?

MR. ACHE *(Putting his hand on his ear.)* Oh, I have an earache. *(To the receptionist.)* This is taking too long. Can I see the doctor now?

RECEPTIONIST *(To Mr. Ache.)* Just a moment, Mr. Ache. *(On the phone.)* And how's Uncle George?... Not very well?... He can't walk, he can't swim, he can't dance... He can't do anything anymore?

MR. ACHE *(Well, but anxious.)* What's wrong with him? What's wrong with him?

RECEPTIONIST *(On the phone.)* He has a terrible backache.

MR. ACHE *(Putting his hands on his back, screams.)* Oh! My back hurts. I can't move!

RECEPTIONIST *(On the phone.)* Poor Uncle George... What?... Sometimes it's difficult for him to breathe?

MR. ACHE *(Breathing with difficulty.)* I can't breathe!... Help me please.

RECEPTIONIST *(On the phone.)* I'm so sorry to hear that... Yes, I'm fine, but I'm very busy. Everybody in this city seems to be sick nowadays. Lots of people have the flu. *(Mr. Ache sneezes. To Mr. Ache.)* Bless you. *(On the phone.)* My roommate has a cough. *(Mr. Ache coughs.)* My neighbor has a fever. *(Mr. Ache puts his hand on his forehead, to see if he has a fever.)* Do you remember Gloria, my friend from the club? She broke an arm. *(Mr. Ache examines his arms desperately.)* And now you won't believe this. My English teacher had a heart attack in the classroom.

MR. ACHE *(Putting his hand on his chest, screams.)* Ahh!!! I'm having a heart attack. Do something, quick! Ahh!

RECEPTIONIST *(On the phone.)* Just a second, Mom. *(Gets some cotton from her drawer and walks towards him.)* Mr. Ache, I have the solution to your problem.

MR. ACHE What?

RECEPTIONIST Cotton. *(She shows it to him.)* Put the cotton in your ear.

MR. ACHE What?

RECEPTIONIST Put the cotton in your ear.

MR. ACHE *(Not understanding.)* Oh, OK. *(Gets the cotton and puts it in his ears.)*

RECEPTIONIST *(To herself.)* Let's try this. *(To him. He doesn't react because he can't hear.)* Earache... Backache... Stomachache... Cough... Flu... Sore throat... Heart attack... *(Takes the cotton from his ears.)* Mr. Ache, you're cured.

MR. ACHE *(Surprised.)* I am?

RECEPTIONIST Yes, you are. You can go home now. Just remember to keep the cotton in your ears.

MR. ACHE I'm cured?

RECEPTIONIST Yes?

MR. ACHE *(Happy, goes out, shouting.)* I'm cured! I'm cured! I'm cured! *(Exits.)*

RECEPTIONIST *(To the door.)* Bye, bye, Mr. Ache. See you next week. *(Goes back to the phone.)* So, Mom... *(The conversation fades.)*

THE END

On Old McDonald's Farm

LEVEL OF ENGLISH: Basic, very simple

RECOMMENDED AGE: Children, ages 7 and above

STRUCTURES:

Grammar: Verb to be in the simple present
Vocabulary: Farm animals

NUMBER OF CHARACTERS: 6 children. You can use any number of characters. Just add or redistribute lines.

COSTUMES: Ordinary clothes. Since the characters are visiting a farm, they can wear caps and sunglasses. They can also carry backpacks. Each of the children should carry a book.

PLAYING TIME: Approximately 5 minutes

SOME SUGGESTIONS:

✷ The animals the children point to can be pictures, stuffed animals or any other toy animals the children may have or make.
✷ You can use this sketch with older children or with children who speak more English. All you have to do is elaborate a little bit on the language.

On Old McDonald's Farm

CHARACTERS *Children 1 to 6*

(The children arrive on the farm. They all carry books.)

CHILD 1 Here we are on a farm.

CHILD 2 It's beautiful.

CHILD 3 It's big.

CHILD 4 It's different.

CHILD 5 Very different.

CHILD 6 Yes. We're city children.

CHILD 1 *(Pointing at a chicken.)* Look! What's that?

CHILD 2 I don't know.

CHILD 3 The book! Look at the book!

(They all look at the book.)

CHILD 4 It's a chicken!

CHILD 5 No, it's a turkey.

CHILD 6 It's a duck.

CHILD 1 Oh, my God! City children... Look at the book again.

(They all look at the book and at the chicken several times.)

CHILD 2 It's a chicken!

CHILD 3 Yes, that's right. It's a chicken.

CHILD 4 *(Pointing at a pig.)* And what's that?

CHILD 5 It's very strange...

CHILD 6 The book! The book! Look at the book!

(They all look at the book.)

CHILD 1 It's a pig.

CHILD 2 No, no, no! It's a horse.

CHILD 3 No, a horse is big.

CHILD 2 Really? *(Looks at the book again.)* Yes. It's a pig.

CHILD 4 What sound does a pig make?

CHILD 5 "Moo."

CHILD 6 No, "cock-a-doodle-doo."

CHILD 1 No, no, no! "Baa baa."

CHILD 2 Look at the book! Look at the book.

(They all look at the book.)

CHILD 3 *(Finds the answer.)* Here! A pig goes "oink oink."

CHILD 4 "Oink oink?"

CHILD 3 Yes, "oink oink."

CHILD 4 Very strange...

CHILD 5 Oh, my God! City children!

CHILD 6 Where are the lions?

CHILD 1 Lions?

CHILD 6 Yes. I want to see the lions.

CHILD 2 The lions are at the zoo!

CHILD 6 At the zoo?

CHILD 3 Yes. This is a farm!

CHILD 4 There are no lions on the farm!

CHILD 6 Very strange...

CHILD 5 _We_ are strange!

CHILD 6 Yes. We're city children...

(They all laugh. Then they all sing.)

ALL Old McDonald had a farm
E-I-E-I-O
And on this farm he had some chicks
E-I-E-I-O
With a cluck-cluck here and a cluck-cluck there
Here a cluck, there a cluck, everywhere a cluck-cluck
Old McDonald had a farm
E-I-E-I-O

Old McDonald had a farm
E-I-E-I-O
And on this farm he had a cow
E-I-E-I-O
With a moo-moo here and a moo-moo there
Here a moo, there a moo, everywhere a moo-moo
Cluck-cluck here and a cluck-cluck there
Here a cluck, there a cluck, everywhere a cluck-cluck
Old McDonald had a farm
E-I-E-I-O

Old McDonald had a farm
E-I-E-I-O
And on this farm he had some ducks
E-I-E-I-O

With a quack-quack here and a quack-quack there
Here a quack, there a quack, everywhere a quack-quack
Moo-moo here and a moo-moo there
Here a moo, there a moo, everywhere a moo-moo
Cluck-cluck here and a cluck-cluck there
Here a cluck, there a cluck, everywhere a cluck-cluck
Old McDonald had a farm
E-I-E-I-O

Old McDonald had a farm
E-I-E-I-O
And on this farm he had some pigs
E-I-E-I-O

With an oink-oink here and an oink-oink there
Here an oink, there an oink, everywhere an oink-oink
Quack-quack here and a quack-quack there
Here a quack, there a quack, everywhere a quack-quack
Moo-moo here and a moo-moo there
Here a moo, there a moo, everywhere a moo-moo
Cluck-cluck here and a cluck-cluck there
Here a cluck, there a cluck, everywhere a cluck-cluck
Old McDonald had a farm
E-I-E-I-O

Old McDonald had a farm
E-I-E-I-O
And on this farm he had a dog
E-I-E-I-O

With a bow-wow here and a bow-wow there
Here a bow, there a wow, everywhere a bow-wow
Oink-oink here and an oink-oink there
Here an oink, there an oink, everywhere an oink-oink
Quack-quack here and a quack-quack there
Here a quack, there a quack, everywhere a quack-quack
Moo-moo here and a moo-moo there
Here a moo, there a moo, everywhere a moo-moo
Cluck-cluck here and a cluck-cluck there
Here a cluck, there a cluck, everywhere a cluck-cluck
Old McDonald had a farm
E-I-E-I-O

THE END

Please Mr. Postman

LEVEL OF ENGLISH: Intermediate

RECOMMENDED AGE: Teenagers and adults

STRUCTURES:

Grammar: Mixed verb tenses, if-clauses (first and second conditionals)
Vocabulary: nothing specific

NUMBER OF CHARACTERS: 4 – Susan, the postman and 2 friends. You can add more friends if you have more actors.

COSTUMES: The girls can wear ordinary clothes. The postman can wear clothes with the same colors as the postman's uniform in your country or in the USA.

PLAYING TIME: Approximately 10 minutes

SOME SUGGESTIONS:

✷ This sketch is based on the song "Please Mr. Postman," by the Carpenters. It might be a good idea to play the song before or after the sketch.
✷ Nowadays it's more politically correct to say "mail carrier" instead of "postman," but we kept the original word because of the lyrics to the song.
✷ Don't give students the whole script. Stop after Betty shouts, "Are you happy now? Are you happy now?" and the postman replies, "But I didn't do anything." Ask students to write an end to the sketch in small groups. Then have each group present their end. At the end of the activity you can show them the end of the story and students can vote for the one they like best.

Please Mr. Postman

CHARACTERS *Postman*
Susan
Jill
Betty

(Susan, Jill and Betty are in front of Susan's house.)

SUSAN *(Pointing.)* Oh, here he comes!

JILL Who?

SUSAN The postman!

JILL Are you expecting any letters?

SUSAN Of course I am. And today I'm sure he'll have something for me.

(The postman enters, singing.)

POSTMAN *(Singing.)* It's a beautiful day in this neighborhood...[1] *(He walks past Susan's house.)*

SUSAN *(To the postman.)* Stop![2]

POSTMAN *(Very nice.)* Yes? Can I help you?

SUSAN Oh, yes, wait a minute, Mr. Postman.

POSTMAN *(Very nice.)* What can I do for you today?

SUSAN Please, Mr. Postman, look and see if there's a letter in your bag for me.

POSTMAN Do you live in this house?

SUSAN *(Anxious.)* Yes. *(Pointing.)* 234 Main Street.

1. This is the opening song of the American TV program "Mr. Rogers' Neighborhood." You can use any song instead.
2. Susan's lines are the words in the song "Please Mr. Postman," by The Carpenters.

POSTMAN *(Without checking.)* I'm sorry, but there's no mail for 234 Main Street today.

SUSAN Can't you check it again, please?

POSTMAN It's not necessary. I've already checked it. I'm sure there's no mail for you.

SUSAN *(Insisting.)* Please, please, Mr. Postman.

POSTMAN Well, if you insist, I can check it again.

(While the postman checks his bag, the girls talk.)

JILL Susan, he's already told you. There's nothing for you.

BETTY Maybe the letter will come tomorrow.

POSTMAN Sorry, but there's nothing here for 234 Main Street.

SUSAN *(Sad.)* Why is it taking such a long time for me to hear from that boy of mine?

JILL Don't be upset, Susan. Maybe he hasn't had enough time to write.

BETTY Wait a little bit more.

POSTMAN *(Sympathetic.)* Yes, maybe I'll bring you good news tomorrow. Bye now. *(Starts exiting.)*

SUSAN *(Stopping him.)* There must be some word today, from my boyfriend so far away.

JILL Susan, don't exaggerate!

BETTY Calm down!

POSTMAN *(Trying to leave.)* See you tomorrow.

SUSAN *(Stopping him again.)* Please Mr. Postman look and see if there's a letter.

POSTMAN *(A little annoyed.)* There are lots of letters here...

SUSAN A letter for me.

BETTY Let's go inside, Susan. Let's watch TV or something.

SUSAN I don't want to watch TV. I want my letter. I know it's inside his bag. But he doesn't want to give it to me. Why is he doing that? Why? *(Starts crying.)*

JILL Susan, this is getting ridiculous!

BETTY Stop crying, Susan. Everybody is looking at us. *(Points to the audience.)*

SUSAN *(Still crying, to the postman.)* I've been standing here waiting, Mr. Postman, so patiently. For just a card or a just a letter saying he's returning home to me.

POSTMAN I'm sorry... I understand how you feel. But there's nothing I can do.

SUSAN *(Crying desperately.)* So many days you pass me by. *(Points to her own eyes.)* See the tears standing in my eyes. You didn't stop to make me feel better, by leaving me a card or a letter.

POSTMAN *(A little angry.)* How can I give you a letter if I don't have one for you?

SUSAN *(Shouting.)* Why don't you check it and see one more time for me?

JILL He already did, Susan.

BETTY Didn't you see him check his bag?

POSTMAN *(Angry.)* Can I go now? *(Starts leaving.)*

SUSAN You got to wait a minute, wait a minute!

JILL *(Shouting.)* Stop, Susan.

POSTMAN What is it now?

SUSAN Come on, deliver the letter! The sooner the better!

POSTMAN *(Angry, shouting.)* I don't have a letter for you! I've already told you!

SUSAN *(Shouts.)* You liar! What are you trying to do to me?

BETTY *(Shaking her.)* Susan, stop! Stop! Stop!

POSTMAN *(To Jill and Betty.)* This woman is crazy! *(To Susan.)* You know what? If I were your boyfriend, I wouldn't write to you, either.

SUSAN What are you trying to say?

JILL Susan! Control yourself!

SUSAN *(To Jill, angry.)* Control myself! I know what you're trying to do! You want to steal my boyfriend! That's why you feel so happy when he doesn't write me letters.

JILL Now you're accusing me?! I'm only trying to help you! I'm your best friend!

SUSAN Best friend, huh? Does your best friend try to steal your boyfriend?

JILL I'm not trying to steal your boyfriend! Why would I want such an ugly boyfriend?

SUSAN Ugly? What do you mean?

JILL Your boyfriend is one of the ugliest men I know.

SUSAN He is not!

JILL He is too!

BETTY *(Embarrassed.)* Jill, control yourself! You're starting to lose control, too.

POSTMAN *(To the audience.)* I can't believe this is happening to me!

SUSAN *(Angry, to Betty.)* Whose side are you on, anyway?

BETTY I'm just trying to help!

SUSAN I know you very well, too. Don't you think I've noticed the way you look at my boyfriend?

BETTY *(Offended.)* What?

POSTMAN *(To the audience.)* These people are crazy!

BETTY *(Very offended.)* How can you say such a thing about me? *(Starts crying.)*

SUSAN Oh, you're such a great actress! Your tears are as false as the color of your hair!

BETTY What? *(Cries more.)*

SUSAN Oh, I'm so unhappy! On the same day I lost my boyfriend, and my two best friends. *(Cries a lot.)*

JILL *(Cries.)* I never thought this was going to happen!

(The three girls cry.)

POSTMAN *(Concerned.)* Can I do anything for you?

JILL *(Angry, to the postman.)* You! This is all your fault! We used to be best friends. Now look at what you've done to us!

POSTMAN *(Surprised.)* Me?

BETTY Yes, you! You're such a bad man! You destroyed a friendship that we've had since we were little girls. *(Shouts.)* Are you happy now? *(Shouts louder.)* Are you happy now?

POSTMAN But I didn't do anything!

SUSAN *(Realizing.)* I know! I know!

JILL & BETTY What?

POSTMAN What?

SUSAN *(Pointing to the postman.)* I know why he's doing that to me. I know why he doesn't want to give me the letter.

JILL & BETTY Why?

POSTMAN Why?

SUSAN *(Happy and romantic.)* He's in love with me.

JILL What?

BETTY Are you crazy? Are you completely nuts?

SUSAN No, I'm not. I can see it in his eyes! His eyes are full of love... *(Grabs the postman. Shouts.)* Admit it! Admit it!

JILL Susan!

POSTMAN *(Confessing.)* She's right. I am really in love with her.

JILL & BETTY *(Very surprised.)* What?

POSTMAN I fell in love with you the first day that I saw you, Susan. I suffered in silence because I knew you had that boyfriend. I was so happy when he traveled, because I knew that it would be my opportunity to be with you. So I made all his letters disappear.

SUSAN *(In love.)* Oh... This is so romantic...

POSTMAN Do you want to be my girlfriend?

SUSAN *(In love.)* Yes...

JILL *(Angry.)* Stop it!

BETTY *(Angry.)* Yes! Stop it!

POSTMAN & SUSAN What?

JILL You can't love her!

BETTY That's right, you can't.

POSTMAN Why not?

SUSAN Yes, why not?

JILL *(To the postman.)* Because I'm in love with you.

BETTY *(Angry, to Jill.)* No, you're not! *(To the postman.)* I'm in love with you.

POSTMAN & SUSAN What?

JILL *(To the postman.)* You're mine!

BETTY *(To Jill.)* No, he's not. *(To the postman.)* You're mine!

POSTMAN *(To the audience.)* I can't believe this is happening. *(To the girls.)* That's enough, ladies. I'm leaving.

JILL No, don't go. You're the love of my life.

BETTY I need you!

POSTMAN I'm getting out of here! *(Exits.)*

SUSAN Don't go!

JILL *(Running after him.)* Come back, my love!

BETTY *(Running after him.)* Love of my life, don't leave me!

SUSAN *(Alone, to the audience.)* Alone again, naturally. *(She sits down and cries.)*

THE END

Rabbit News Program

LEVEL OF ENGLISH: Basic

RECOMMENDED AGE: Children, ages 5 to 12

STRUCTURES:

Grammar: Simple present and simple past
Vocabulary: Easter Vocabulary

NUMBER OF CHARACTERS: Around 10 characters. You can have many actors or have one actor play more than one part.

COSTUMES: All characters in the sketch are rabbits. They should all wear rabbit ears and a rabbit tail. They can wear ordinary clothes on top of that – suits, dresses, pants, hats, etc. If you want the actors to wear masks, don't let them wear masks that cover their faces, or the audience won't be able to see their facial expressions.

PLAYING TIME: Approximately 5 minutes

SOME SUGGESTIONS:

* On one side of the stage place a desk and two chairs, where the anchors will sit. On the other side the different scenes of the news program will appear. If you're working with lights, just turn the lights of that side off while the anchors are speaking – this way the next characters can get ready.
* You can use recorded sound effects for the weather forecast, or ask a group of students to perform the sounds.
* Add other news stories related to what's happening in your city or country at the moment. You can ask your students to give you ideas.
* You can use this play for Easter celebrations. You can also use other animals instead of rabbits. Another possibility is to use ETs and have news stories that are very similar to what's happening in your country now.

Rabbit News Program

CHARACTERS *Anchors 1 and 2*
Bunnies 1 to 4
Peter Rabbitson
Weather Bunny
Britney Rabbitspears
Rabbits

(We hear music from a popular TV news program.)[1]

ANCHOR 1 Good morning. It's 6:20 pm. Oh, in that case, good evening. I'm Bunny Bonner.[2]

ANCHOR 2 And I'm Bunny Bernardes, and this is the news for today. Next week we're celebrating Easter.

ANCHOR 1 Our reporter, Bunny Garcia[3] is on the streets talking to some rabbits. Hello, Bunny Garcia. Hello, Bunny Garcia. Can you hear me?

BUNNY 1 *(In the streets.)* Hello, Bunny Bonner. I'm here on the streets of Rabbitland. I'm very happy to be here. Now I'm going to interview some rabbits. What's your name?

BUNNY 2 Bunny Silva.

BUNNY 1 Do you like Easter?

BUNNY 2 Yes, I do.

BUNNY 1 What do you eat at Easter?

BUNNY 2 I eat chocolate.

BUNNY 1 Thank you.

BUNNY 2 You're welcome. *(Exits.)*

BUNNY 1 *(Talking to another rabbit.)* Excuse me. Can you answer some questions?

BUNNY 3 Sure.

1. Play the opening song of a famous news program in your area.
2. Use the last name of a famous anchorperson in your country.
3. Use the last name of a famous reporter in your country.

BUNNY 1 What's your name?

BUNNY 3 Bunny Smith.

BUNNY 1 Do you like Easter?

BUNNY 3 Oh, yes, I love it.

BUNNY 1 What do you eat at Easter?

BUNNY 3 Well, I eat chocolate!

BUNNY 1 Thank you.

BUNNY 4 My pleasure.

BUNNY 1 *(Talking to another rabbit.)* Excuse me. Can I ask you some questions?

BUNNY 4 I'm sorry, I'm busy.

BUNNY 1 Only a few questions.

BUNNY 4 OK, but be fast. I'm in a hurry.

BUNNY 1 What's your name?

BUNNY 4 Bunny Souza.

BUNNY 1 Do you like Easter?

BUNNY 4 Of course I do. Easter is my favorite holiday.

BUNNY 1 What do you eat at Easter?

BUNNY 4 Chocolate, of course! What a question!

BUNNY 1 Well, thank you.

BUNNY 4 OK. Sorry, I have to go now. *(Exits quickly.)*

BUNNY 1 OK, Bunny Bonner. Back to you in the studio.

ANCHOR 1 Thank you, Bunny Garcia. Our conclusion is rabbits eat chocolate at Easter. They don't eat carrots.

ANCHOR 2 And now, Hollywood. Yesterday in Hollywood there was a great celebration – the Oscarrot. The best movie was "The Lord of the Carrots."[4] And now let's watch a scene from this wonderful movie.

4. Use the name of the last movie that got the Oscar and add something related to rabbits.

(Some rabbits imitate a scene from the movie very badly.)

ANCHOR 1 Peter Rabbitson[5] got the Oscarrot for best director for that film. And now, let's watch Peter Rabbitson receiving his Oscarrot.

RABBITS ON Thank you very much. I'd like to thank the Academy. And thank you, my mother. Thank you, Father. Thank you, Brother. Thank you, Sister. Thank you, Grandmother. Thank you, Grandfather... *(Is cut off by music. Shouts.)* I haven't finished! I haven't finished!

ANCHOR 2 And now, the weather forecast, with the Weather Bunny.

WEATHER *(Shows charts.)* And this is the weather in Rabbitland. It's hot and sunny. It's hot and sunny in the south, it's hot and sunny in the west... *(We hear wind. The Weather Bunny changes the chart.)* It's windy! It's very windy in Rabbitland today... *(We hear thunder and rain.)* No, no, no. It's rainy! It's rainy! Well, if you want to know what the weather is like, look out your window! Back to you, Bunny Bonner.

ANCHOR 1 Thank you, Weather Bunny. Britney Rabbitspears[6] in Rabbitland. The great pop star Britney Rabbitspears arrived yesterday. She's staying at the Bunny Plaza Hotel.[7] Tomorrow she's going to sing at Bunnycard Hall.[8] And here's a scene from her last show in New York City.

(We see a scene from Britney Rabbitspears's show.)

ANCHOR 2 And that's all for today. We'll be back tomorrow. Good bye.

ANCHOR 1 Good bye.

(Lights fade on Anchors. We hear music from the news program.)

THE END

5. Use the name of the last director or actor who got the Oscar and add something related to rabbits.

6. Use the name of a famous singer and add something related to rabbits.

7. Use the name of a famous hotel and add something related to rabbits.

8. Use the name of a place where shows are presented in your city and add something related to rabbits.

School for Fish

LEVEL OF ENGLISH: Basic

RECOMMENDED AGE: Children (ages 10 and above) and teenagers

STRUCTURES:

Grammar: Although other verb tenses appear, the focus is on the simple present.
Vocabulary: Parts of the body, differences between fish and humans

NUMBER OF CHARACTERS: 11 – a teacher and 10 students. The number of students can be changed to suit the group of actors you have.

COSTUMES: All the characters are fish. Use you imagination to create the costumes. If you want the actors to wear masks, don't let them wear masks that cover their faces, or the audience won't be able to see their facial expressions.

PLAYING TIME: Between 5 and 10 minutes

SOME SUGGESTIONS:

✷ The story takes place at an under the sea school. You can place pictures of fish on the walls to create the atmosphere.
✷ The students can sit on the floor and the teacher can stand.
✷ At the end of the sketch you can sing a song about the sea.
✷ In English students don't address the teacher by the word "teacher." They use his or her first name or last name (John or Mr. Brown). Call students' attention to that.

School for Fish[1]

CHARACTERS *Teacher, a fish*
Students 1 to 10, fishes

(The story takes place at an under the sea school. The students are together. The teacher enters.)

TEACHER Good morning, everybody.

STUDENTS Good morning.

TEACHER How are you?

STUDENTS Fine, thanks. And you?

TEACHER I'm fine, thank you.

STUDENT 1 I'm very excited today!

TEACHER Really? Why?

STUDENT 1 Because today we're going to study humans.

TEACHER Yes. You remembered that, right?

STUDENTS Right!

STUDENT 2 How could we forget?

STUDENT 3 You said you'd show us many human objects...

TEACHER Yes, that's right. So are you ready to start the class?

STUDENTS Yes!

TEACHER Well, the first big difference between humans and fish is that fish swim and humans walk.

STUDENT 4 Walk? What's that?

TEACHER Well, they have legs and they move their legs and walk. Like this. *(Walks in a funny way.)*

1. Inspired by a dialog from the movie "The Little Mermaid."

STUDENTS Oh...

TEACHER But this is not all.

STUDENT 5 There's more?

TEACHER Yes. There's a lot more...

STUDENT 6 What?

TEACHER Well, humans use their noses to breathe.

STUDENT 7 Don't they have gills?

TEACHER No, they don't.

STUDENTS Oh...

STUDENT 8 That's amazing!

STUDENT 9 *(Excited.)* What else? What else?

TEACHER They don't have scales. They have hair.

STUDENT 10 Oh, come on. Everybody has scales.

TEACHER Not everybody. Humans, for example, don't have scales.

STUDENT 10 But my father told me that everybody has scales...

TEACHER I'm sorry, but humans don't. I'm a teacher and I know many things. I don't know everything, but I know many things. And I'm sure humans don't have scales.

STUDENT 10 OK. I'm sorry...

TEACHER Well, let's continue. Let me show you some human objects.

STUDENT 1 Oh, my Neptune![2] I'm so excited...

TEACHER Look at this. *(Shows a fork.)*

STUDENT 2 What's this?

TEACHER It's an oozit.[3] Repeat everybody, "It's an oozit."

STUDENTS It's an oozit.

STUDENT 3 What do humans do with oozits?

2. This is equivalent to "Oh, my God!" since Neptune is the god of the seas.
3. This is not a real word. You can use any word with a funny sound.

TEACHER They comb their hair.

STUDENTS They comb their hair?

TEACHER Yes, that's right. They comb their hair. Like this. *(Combs her hair with the fork.)*

STUDENTS Oh...

STUDENT 4 Are you sure?

TEACHER Yes. I'm a teacher and I know many things. I don't know *everything*, but I know many things.

STUDENT 5 *(To another student.)* Wow! Our teacher is really smart. *(To the teacher.)* What else do you have?

TEACHER Look at this. *(Shows a sock.)*

STUDENT 6 It's beautiful. What is it?

TEACHER It's a whazzit. Repeat everybody, "It's a whazzit."

STUDENTS It's a whazzit.

STUDENT 7 *(Holding it.)* It smells funny...

STUDENT 8 What is it for?

TEACHER Well, I read in a book that humans used whazzits to keep their tails warm.

STUDENTS Oh...

STUDENT 9 I didn't know humans had tails.

TEACHER Oh, they do. But nobody can see their tails.

STUDENT 10 Why not?

TEACHER Because they wear clothes. The tails are hidden under their clothes.

STUDENTS Oh...

STUDENT 1 Are you sure?

TEACHER Of course. I'm a teacher and I know many things. I don't know *everything*, but I know many things.

STUDENT 2 But if their tails are hidden under their clothes, why do they need those... what are they called...uh... whazzits to keep their tails warm?

TEACHER That's a very good question. But I don't know the answer.

STUDENTS You don't?

TEACHER No. As I said before I know many things, but I don't know *everything*. I'll answer that next class.

STUDENT 3 Show us more!

STUDENT 4 More, please!

TEACHER OK. Now I'm going to show you a very beautiful object that humans use.

STUDENTS What?

TEACHER Look at this? *(Shows a hook.)*

STUDENT 5 What is this?

TEACHER It's a shook. Repeat everybody, "It's a shook."

STUDENTS It's a shook.

STUDENT 6 What's a shook for?

TEACHER Humans use it to hang their clothes.

STUDENT 7 To hang their clothes. Really?

STUDENT 8 Are you sure?

TEACHER Yes. I'm a teacher and I know many things. I don't know *everything*, but I know many things.

STUDENT 9 Excuse me, but I know this object. It's not a shook, it's a hook.

TEACHER A hook?

STUDENT 9 Yes, and it's not used to hang clothes. It's used to catch fish.

STUDENTS *(Scared.)* What?

TEACHER *(Very scared.)* To catch fish? Oh, my Neptune! Aaaah!! Help! Help! Help! *(Runs out.)*

STUDENT 10 Well, she certainly knows many things, but she doesn't know *everything*!

(All the students laugh.)

THE END

The Big Bad Wolf's School

LEVEL OF ENGLISH: Intermediate

RECOMMENDED AGE: Children ages 8 to 12

STRUCTURES:

Grammar: Mixed verb tenses
Vocabulary: related to the Big Bad Wolf's stories

NUMBER OF CHARACTERS: 10 – The reporter, the Big Bad Wolf and 8 students. The number of students can be changed. The students' lines are easier than the reporter's and the Big Bad Wolf's.

COSTUMES: The reporter can wear formal clothes and hold a microphone. The Big Bad Wolf and the students can wear long ears and a tail sticking out of their clothes. If they wear masks, choose half-masks that cover only the top of their heads – it's important for an actor to show his face, so he can show his emotions.

PLAYING TIME: Approximately 8 minutes

SOME SUGGESTIONS:

- You don't need any special setting for this sketch. You can write a card with the words "Big Bad Wolf's School" and place it on the wall. You can have a classroom setting, with chairs and desks, or you can have everybody standing, as if they were in front of the school.
- You can record a howling sound and play it when the wolves howl.
- You can ask students to write a similar story using other characters.

THE BIG BAD WOLF'S SCHOOL

CHARACTERS *Reporter*
Big Bad Wolf
Students 1 to 8

(The reporter is standing next to the Big Bad Wolf and his students. He speaks to the audience as if he were speaking to the camera.)

REPORTER Hello, everybody. Super English School TV[1] presents a special news program. We're going to interview a very famous person – the Big Bad Wolf. Yes, the famous Big Bad Wolf from many fairy tales is going to talk to us today. The big news is that he opened a school – The Big Bad Wolf's School. And we're here in his school to talk to him and some of his students. *(To Big Bad Wolf.)* Hello, Big Bad Wolf. Welcome to our program.

WOLF Thank you. It's a pleasure to be here. *(Howls.)*

REPORTER And these are the students in the Big Bad Wolf's School.

STUDENTS Hi. *(They wave.)*

REPORTER Do you like the Big Bad Wolf's school?

STUDENTS *(Cheering.)* Yes!

REPORTER Tell us, Big Bad Wolf, why did you decide to open this school?

WOLF Well, I'm a great Big Bad Wolf. I'm famous. I'm in many different stories. I have a lot of experience and I'd like to share it with younger wolves.

REPORTER I see...

WOLF Also, I'm getting a little old and I have to prepare a new generation of Big Bad Wolves. People will always need us in their stories. We're very important, right, kids?

STUDENTS *(Cheering.)* Right!

REPORTER We can see your students really like you.

WOLF Like? They adore me! I'm the great, the wonderful, the fabulous *Big Bad Wolf*!

1. Use the name of your school, or the name of a TV station in your area.

STUDENTS *(Cheering.)* Yes!

REPORTER So, what do you teach in your school?

WOLF Many things.

REPORTER What kinds of things?

WOLF Things that are important for someone to be a Big Bad Wolf.

REPORTER Yes. Can you give us an example?

WOLF Well, we start with very simple lessons. We always start with howling. *(Howls.)*

REPORTER Why?

WOLF It's very important for a Big Bad Wolf to howl well. This is how he can scare other people. *(Howls.)*

REPORTER How do you teach a student how to howl?

WOLF First you have to have the right posture. *(He does it as he speaks.)* Bend your knees a little bit, lean your chest forward, move your neck up, close your fists very tightly and go, "A-ooh."

REPORTER It sounds a little difficult.

WOLF It's a little difficult at first, but practice makes perfect. You have to practice, practice, practice. Let me show you one of my beginner students. *(Points to Student 1.)* Come here.

STUDENT 1 Yes, Big Bad Wolf?

WOLF Show him how you can howl.

STUDENT 1 I'll try.

WOLF Yes. Try it. Trying is very important for you to learn.

STUDENT 1 *(Howls very softly.)* A-ooh.

WOLF *(To Student 1.)* It was very good. With practice it will be much better.

STUDENT 1 Thank you.

WOLF *(To Student 2.)* Now come here. *(To the reporter.)* This is one of my advanced students.

STUDENT 2 Yes, Big Bad Wolf?

WOLF Show him how you can howl.

STUDENT 2 Yes, Big Bad Wolf. *(Howls very loudly.)* A-ooh!

WOLF *(To Student 2.)* Excellent. With practice it will be even better.

STUDENT 2 Thanks.

WOLF *(To the reporter.)* See? The most important thing in learning is practice.

REPORTER Thanks for the demonstration. What else do you teach your students?

WOLF Well, blowing is something very important for a Big Bad Wolf.

REPORTER Blowing? Why?

WOLF Well, sometimes we need to huff and puff and blow houses in. Don't you remember my stories?

REPORTER Yes, of course. So, how do you teach them how to blow?

WOLF Well, we start with very simple things. We use a piece of paper to start with.

REPORTER How interesting...

WOLF *(To the students.)* Get your pieces of paper. *(They all get a piece of paper.)* Open and close your mouths many times. *(They do it. To the reporter.)* It's important to warm up first. *(To the students.)* Now blow. *(They hold the pieces of paper with both hands, place them in front of their mouths and blow many times.)* Good. More energy. *(They blow harder.)* Excellent! Now let the pieces of paper go. *(They let go of the pieces of paper and they fly away.)* Very good, guys.

REPORTER And then?

WOLF Well, blowing pieces of paper is just the beginning. Then we move on to heavier things – books, chairs, tables, doors, etc, until they're able to blow a house in. Then we move on to bigger things – buildings, shopping centers, cities...

REPORTER Oh, my! Isn't that hard?

WOLF Hard? No, that's very easy. All you need is more air and a lot of concentration.

REPORTER That's really fantastic. What else do your students learn here?

WOLF Another important lesson for a Big Bad Wolf is how to swallow big things in one piece.

REPORTER That must be difficult.

WOLF Well, we start with small things and then get bigger and bigger things.

REPORTER Can you give us an example?

WOLF *(To the students.)* Can you tell him the things you've learned how to swallow in one piece?

STUDENT 3 Grapes.

STUDENT 4 Eggs.

STUDENT 5 Oranges.

STUDENT 6 Melons.

STUDENT 7 Watermelons.

STUDENT 8 Babies.

STUDENT 1 Little girls.

STUDENT 2 Grandmothers.

REPORTER *(Afraid.)* Wow... And what else do they learn?

WOLF Well, a lot of things. *(To the students.)* Tell him some of the things you learn here.

STUDENT 3 We have cooking lessons.

STUDENT 4 We learn how to cook pork in many different ways.

STUDENT 5 We learn how to climb houses.

STUDENT 6 And how to go down chimneys.

REPORTER Isn't that dangerous?

STUDENT 7 Dangerous? Not at all.

STUDENT 8 We wear protection.

REPORTER Protection? Like what?

WOLF *(To the reporter.)* Well, this is still a secret, but I invented a protective suit against hot water. It will be very useful for Big Bad Wolves.

REPORTER That's good news... for Big Bad Wolves... Well, we have very little time left. I'd like to thank you once again for talking to Super English School TV.

WOLF You're welcome.

REPORTER Before we finish, I'd like to ask your students a few questions.

WOLF Go ahead.

REPORTER *(To the students.)* So, kids, do you like to study in this school?

STUDENT 1 Yes, I like it very much.

STUDENT 2 The school is excellent.

STUDENT 3 We learn a lot.

REPORTER And is the Big Bad Wolf a good teacher?

STUDENT 4 Yes, he is.

STUDENT 5 He's an excellent teacher.

STUDENT 6 He's very patient.

STUDENT 7 And he knows a lot.

STUDENT 8 He knows everything. Of course, he's the Big Bad Wolf!

REPORTER So you all love the Big Bad Wolf.

STUDENTS Yes, we do.

REPORTER Aren't you afraid of him?

STUDENTS Of course not! Who's afraid of the Big Bad Wolf? *(They laugh.)*

REPORTER *(To the audience.)* That's the end of our fantastic interview with the Big Bad Wolf. Thank you for watching and good bye!

THE END

The English Student

LEVEL OF ENGLISH: Basic

RECOMMENDED AGE: Teenagers and adults

STRUCTURES:

Grammar: Simple present
Vocabulary: Vocabulary used in introductions and talking about oneself

NUMBER OF CHARACTERS: 2 – Paulo and Helga

COSTUMES: Paulo can wear ordinary clothes. Since he's Brazilian, he can wear the colors of the Brazilian flag, or a T-shirt with a picture of the Brazilian flag. If you change his nationality, change the colors of his clothes accordingly. Helga can wear ordinary clothes.

PLAYING TIME: Approximately 5 minutes

SOME SUGGESTIONS:

- Use two chairs side by side to pretend it's a bench in a park.
- If you're doing it in the classroom, draw some trees on the blackboard and place the bench in front of it. You can also draw trees on cardboard paper and stick them to the walls.
- Paulo should have a discman. This has to be clear for the audience, but not for Helga. If you prefer, you can hide the discman from the audience, too, so they will notice it when Helga does.

The English Student

CHARACTERS *Paulo, a Brazilian student*
Helga, a German woman

(A park in the United States. Paulo enters, sits on a bench, gets a discman, shows it to the audience, puts his earphones on, and turns the discman on. Helga enters and sits next to him.)

PAULO *(Repeating after the recording.)* Hello! *(Helga looks around.)* Hello!

HELGA *(Thinking he's talking to her.)* Hello.

PAULO What's your name?

HELGA My name is Helga. And yours?

PAULO My name is Donald Logan. L – O – G – A – N. Logan.

HELGA Hi, Donald.

PAULO My name's Ted Clark.

HELGA Oh, sorry. I thought you said Donald.

PAULO Nice to meet you, Ted.

HELGA *(Confused.)* Sorry?

PAULO Nice to meet you, Donald.

HELGA No, I thought *your* name was Donald. My name is Helga.

PAULO Where are you from?

HELGA I'm from Germany.

PAULO I'm from the United States. I'm American. Are you American?

HELGA No, I'm German. What city are you from?

PAULO Yes, I'm American.

HELGA I know that, but what *city* are you from?

PAULO I'm from Springfield.

HELGA Springfield? Where's that?

PAULO Springfield is in Colorado.

HELGA Ah!

PAULO Where are you from?

HELGA I'm from Frankfurt.

PAULO I'm from Springfield.

HELGA You've already told me. *(Grins.)*

PAULO What a coincidence!

HELGA What?

PAULO We are both from Springfield.

HELGA *(Losing her patience.)* I'm from Frankfurt. *(Paulo listens to the recording and mouths some words.)* Excuse me? Can you speak louder?

PAULO That's Terry.

HELGA *(Looking around.)* Where?

PAULO She is from Brazil.

HELGA Is she your friend?

PAULO *She's* from Brazil.

HELGA I understand.

PAULO Park.

HELGA *(Looking around.)* Yeah, this is a park.

PAULO Pot... Pen... Picture... Person...

HELGA *(She doesn't understand anything.)* Are you OK? *(He mouths some words again.)* What? I can't understand.

PAULO Are you busy?

HELGA No, what about you?

PAULO No, I'm not.

HELGA Why do you ask?

PAULO Would you like to go out?

HELGA Are you asking me out on a date?

PAULO Sure. Where would you like to go?

HELGA *(Flattered.)* Well, I don't know...

PAULO How about going to the movies?

HELGA Well, there's a movie theater around the corner.

PAULO Good idea.

HELGA Let's go then.

PAULO What kind of movies do you like?

HELGA I like comedies.

PAULO I like romantic movies.

HELGA I love romantic movies. I'm very romantic.

PAULO Me too.

HELGA That's nice.

PAULO Have you seen "Love Story?"

HELGA Many times. Have you seen "Love Actually?"

PAULO No, I haven't. Is it good?

HELGA It's beautiful. Let's watch it then.

PAULO It's a very famous movie.

HELGA I know.

PAULO OK, then. Let's go.

HELGA All right. *(Stands up. He doesn't move.)* Let's. *(He stares in the distance. He mouths some words. She doesn't understand anything. She pokes him.)* Are you OK?

PAULO *(Taking off the earphones.)* What?

HELGA What's up?

PAULO *(Looks up to the sky.)* Where?

HELGA No, I mean, are you OK?

PAULO Who are you?

HELGA *(Not understanding.)* I'm Helga, from Germany. We've been talking for ten minutes.

PAULO *(Not understanding.)* Talking? I was here alone studying English. *(Shows her the discman.)*

HELGA *(Realizing, feeling dumb.)* Oh, you're a student! I'm sorry.

PAULO That's OK. Hi, I'm Paulo. I'm from Brazil.

HELGA Nice to meet you, Paulo. I'm Helga. I'm from Germany.

(They shake hands.)

PAULO Nice to meet you, too.

HELGA So, what are you studying?

PAULO Well, this is my first time here in the United States. I'm a little shy and I'm trying to learn how to invite a girl to go on a date with me.

HELGA Well, I have good news for you.

PAULO What is it?

HELGA You *are* going on a date... with *me*.

PAULO *(Happy.)* I am?

HELGA *(Pushing him.)* Yes, let's go to the movies.

PAULO *(Very happy, kissing his discman, to the audience.)* Wow! It works! *(They exit.)*

THE END

The ETs

LEVEL OF ENGLISH: Basic, with very simple structures and Vocabulary

RECOMMENDED AGE: Children, from 5 years old

STRUCTURES:

Grammar: What's this?/It's a __./It's an __.
Vocabulary: Objects

NUMBER OF CHARACTERS: 12 – 6 ETs and 6 people. This number can be modified. You can have fewer characters and assign more lines to each one. You can have more characters and assign fewer lines to each one. You can create your own lines and show different objects. Use your imagination. You will need at least 2 people and 1 ET.

COSTUMES: Ordinary clothes for the people and funny clothes for the ETs.

PLAYING TIME: About 5 minutes

SOME SUGGESTIONS:

- You don't need a spaceship to perform this play. To show the audience that the spaceship is landing, have the people look up and then look down slowly. Then have the ETs enter the scene.
- To represent the school, use a table and place some objects on top of it. The walls and the door of the school can be imaginary.
- If your students can't read yet, teach them one line at a time. Then have them repeat the whole sketch from the beginning (or as we say in theater, "from the top.")
- At the end of the sketch, all characters can sing the song "Hello, Goodbye," by The Beatles, or any other song that has the words "Hello" and "Good bye."

The ETs

CHARACTERS *People 1 to 6*
ETs 1 to 6

(The people are outside. They hear a strange sound. They look up and see a spaceship landing.)

PERSON 1 What's that?

PERSON 2 I don't know.

PERSON 3 Is it a bird?

PERSON 4 No, it isn't.

PERSON 5 Is it a plane?

PERSON 6 No, it isn't.

PERSON 1 It's a spaceship!

PEOPLE *(Surprised.)* A spaceship?

PERSON 2 Impossible!

(The ETs enter.)

ET 1 Do you speak English?

PERSON 3 Yes, we do.

ET 2 We are from Planet Borgg.

ET 3 We are friends.

PERSON 4 Welcome to our planet.

ET 4 Can you show us your planet?

PERSON 5 Of course.

PERSON 6 Come with us.

(They start walking. They see a school.)

ET 5 What's this?

PEOPLE It's a school.

ETs *(Surprised.)* A school?

PERSON 1 Yes, it's a school.

(They enter the school.)

ET 6 *(Gets a pencil and shows it.)* What's this?

PERSON 2 It's a pencil.

ETs *(Surprised.)* A pencil?

ET 1 On Borgg this is a banana.

PEOPLE *(Surprised.)* A banana?

(They all laugh.)

ET 2 *(Gets a book.)* What's this?

PERSON 3 It's a book.

ETs *(Surprised.)* A book?

ET 3 On Borgg this is a car.

PEOPLE *(Surprised.)* A car?

(They all laugh.)

ET 4 *(Pointing to a chair.)* What's this?

PERSON 4 It's a chair.

ETs *(Surprised.)* A chair?

ET 5 On Borgg this is a ball.

PEOPLE *(Surprised.)* A ball?

(They all laugh.)

ET 6 Do you have a family?

PEOPLE Yes, we do.

PERSON 5 We have a father, a mother, brothers and sisters.

ETs *(Surprised.)* *One* father and *one* mother?

ET 1 On Borgg we have 3 fathers and 4 mothers.

PEOPLE *(Surprised.)* 3 fathers and 4 mothers?

(They all laugh.)

ET 2 Well, time to go.

ET 3 Thank you.

PEOPLE You're welcome.

PERSON 6 Come back some day.

PERSON 1 Goodbye.

ET 4 Hello!

PEOPLE Goodbye!

ETs Hello!

PERSON 2 Here we say goodbye!

ETs *(Surprised.)* Goodbye?

ET 5 On Borgg we say Hello!

PEOPLE *(Surprised.)* Hello?

(They all laugh. The ETs exit.)

THE END

The Fight

LEVEL OF ENGLISH: Basic

RECOMMENDED AGE: Children, ages 6 and above

STRUCTURES:

Grammar: Simple present
Vocabulary: Words with the letters K and X

NUMBER OF CHARACTERS: 11 – The Master of Ceremonies, the letter K, the letter X, 4 K fans and 4 X fans. You can change the number of fans and redistribute the lines accordingly. You can also have a coach for each letter, instead of the fans.

COSTUMES: Letter K should wear red shorts, and a white T-shirt with the letter K on it. Letter X should wear blue shorts and a white T-shirt with the letter X on it. The fans can wear ordinary clothes with the letters they support written on the shirts. The MC can wear more elegant clothes. The MC should have a bell.

PLAYING TIME: Approximately 5 minutes

SOME SUGGESTIONS:

* You don't need special scenery for this play.
* The fans can carry posters with the letters they support written on them.
* The sketch has to look like a real boxing match. The more violent it is, the funnier it will be. However, the contestants fight with words. They don't touch each other.
* At the end they can all sing songs that mention the letters K and X.
* You can use the same idea and write different sketches with different letters, or different word categories.

The Fight

CHARACTERS *MC – The Master of Ceremonies*
K
X
K Fans 1 to 4
X Fans 1 to 4

MC And now here's the fight of the century. On the right, wearing blue shorts, and a white T-shirt, the letter X!

X FANS Yeah!!

X FAN 1 X is the best!

X FAN 2 It's my favorite letter!

X FAN 3 It's sensational!

X FAN 4 We love it!

X FANS Letter X! Letter X! Letter X!

X Thank you, my fans!

MC On the left, wearing red shorts, and a white T-shirt, the letter K!

K FANS K-K! This letter is OK!

K FAN 1 K is wonderful!

K FAN 2 K is beautiful!

K FAN 3 K is better than X!

K FAN 4 K is the best!

K FANS K-K! This letter is OK!

K I know I'm the best. I'm going to win this fight!

X Let's just wait and see!

MC First round! You have to say words that begin with "K" and "X." Are you ready?

K & X Yes.

MC Start! *(Rings the bell.)*

(K and X look and each other and shout. They fight with words.)

K *(Angry.)* Kitchen!

X *(Angry.)* Xerox!

K *(Angry.)* Kite!

X *(Angry.)* Xylophone!

K *(Attacking.)* Kitten!

X *(Hesitating.)* Uh... uh...

X FAN 1 Come on, "X!"

X FAN 2 Don't stop now!

X FAN 3 You can win!

X FAN 4 Think!

X I don't know.

MC *(Rings the bell.)* One point for the letter "K."

K FANS K-K! This letter is OK!

MC Let's start the second round! In this round you have to say words that finish with "K" and "X." Are you ready?

K & X Ready!

MC Start! *(Rings the bell.)*

X *(Shouts.)* Six!

K *(Shouts.)* Sock!

X *(Shouts.)* Box!

K *(Shouts.)* Homework!

X *(Shouts.)* Mix!

K *(Shouts.)* Book!

X *(Shouts.)* Fox!

K *(Hesitating.)* Uh... uh...

K FAN 1 Keep going!

K FAN 2 You are doing well!

K FAN 3 We believe in you!

K FAN 4 We really do!

K I don't know!

K FANS Oh!!

MC *(Rings the bell.)* One point for the letter "X."

X FANS Yeah! X! X! X! Yeah!

MC And now the third round. You have to say words that have the letters "X" and "K" in the middle. Are you ready?

X & K Yes!

MC Start! *(Rings the bell.)*

K *(Angry.)* Jacket!

X *(Angry.)* Texas!

K *(Angry.)* Chicken!

X *(Angry.)* Excellent!

K *(Angry.)* Rollerskates!

X *(Angry.)* Mexico!

K *(Angry.)* Rocket!

X *(Angry.)* Expensive!

K *(Angry.)* Monkey!

X *(Angry.)* Taxi!

MC *(Rings the bell.)* Time is up! One point for the letter "X" and one point for the letter "K."

X FANS Yeah! X! X! X!

K FANS K-K! This letter is OK!

MC There are no winners. It's a tie! Now let's celebrate!

(They all celebrate.)

THE END

The Joe Puppy Program

LEVEL OF ENGLISH: Basic

RECOMMENDED AGE: Children, ages 8 and above

STRUCTURES:

Grammar: Simple present
Vocabulary: Occupations, Days of the week

NUMBER OF CHARACTERS: 7 – Joe Puppy (the host), Super Dog and 5 Puppies (the singers). You can change the number of singers in the band and divide the lines accordingly. You can also create more lines. You can add some dancers in the band. They can have more lines or they can simply dance.

COSTUMES: All characters in the sketch are dogs. Students can wear dog ears and tails and put on dog make up. The host can wear clothes that make him look like a real talk-show host. Super Dog can wear a Superman costume (or similar) substituting the "S" for an "SD." The members of the band can wear leather jackets and sunglasses trying to look like real rock stars. If they wear masks, choose half-masks that cover only the top of their heads – it's important for an actor to show his face, so he can show his emotions.

PLAYING TIME: Approximately 10 minutes

SOME SUGGESTIONS:

✷ You can have a chair and a desk for the host and a chair for the guest, or you can have them stand on stage.
✷ The more the sketch looks like an actual talk show that everybody knows, the funnier it will be. The characters in this play are dogs, but you can use any other animal such as rabbits (if you're celebrating Easter for example), cats, or even people.

THE JOE PUPPY PROGRAM[1]

CHARACTERS Joe Puppy
Super Dog
The Puppies

(Music.[2] Joe Puppy[3] enters.)

JOE Hello, hello. Welcome to "The Joe Puppy Program." Our guest today is a special dog. He looks like a normal dog, but everybody calls him Super Dog. He's going to tell us why. Here's Super Dog.

(Super Dog enters. He's holding a box full of hats.)

SUPER Good evening.

JOE So, Super Dog, can you tell us why your name is Super Dog?

SUPER Can I just say, Joe, for one moment, why my name is Super Dog?

JOE Exactly. Tell us about it.

SUPER What?

JOE Your name.

SUPER Oh, my name.

JOE Yes.

SUPER Oh, my name. Well, Joe, you can ask me about my name.

1. Inspired by the sketch "Anne Elk," by Monty Python.
2. It's a good idea to record the opening song of an actual talk-show that is popular on TV.
3. Jô Soares is a famous talk-show host in Brazil. This sketch is a parody of his program. You can change the name of the program and the name of the host to a famous name in your country. For example, the name of the host can be "Dog Letterman" and the name of the show could be "The Late Dog Show."

JOE I am asking.

SUPER Good for you. Well, Joe, my name is Super Dog.

JOE *(Beginning to show exasperation.)* Yes, I know it's Super Dog. Why is your name Super Dog?

SUPER Why? Oh, why my name is Super Dog... This is it. *(Clears throat.)* My name is Super Dog because... *(Clears throat.)* Now I'm going to say why my name is Super Dog. Ready?

JOE Yes.

SUPER *(Clears throat.)* My name is Super Dog, because I have many different jobs.

JOE Many different jobs?

SUPER Yes. I have a different job every day.

JOE Well, this is very interesting.

SUPER Yes, it is.

JOE What do you do on Monday?

SUPER On Monday I'm a firefighter. *(Puts on a firefighter's hat.)*

JOE Where do you work?

SUPER I work at the fire station.

JOE What do you do?

SUPER I fight fires. I drive the fire engine. I shout, "Fire, fire!" I help dogs. It's very exciting.

JOE What do you do on Tuesday?

SUPER On Tuesday I'm a police officer. *(Puts on a police officer's hat.)*

JOE A police officer? Where do you work?

SUPER I work at the police station. I work on the street.

JOE What do you do?

SUPER I help dogs, I take care of the traffic. I look for robbers.

JOE Very nice. And what do you do on Wednesday?

SUPER I'm a cook. *(Puts on a cook's hat.)*

JOE Really? Where do you work?

SUPER At the restaurant, of course.

JOE And what do you do?

SUPER I cook... of course.

JOE Of course... What do you do on Thursday?

SUPER On Thursday I'm a farmer. *(Puts on a farmer's hat.)*

JOE Where do you work?

SUPER I work on my farm. I feed the animals, I take care of the plants and flowers.

JOE What do you do on Friday?

SUPER On Friday I'm a sailor. *(Puts on a sailor's hat.)*

JOE A sailor? Where do you work?

SUPER On my boat.

JOE What do you do?

SUPER *(Sings.)* Row, row, row, your boat, gently down the stream, merrily, merrily, merrily, merrily life is but a dream.

JOE What do you do on Saturday, Super Dog?

SUPER On Saturday I'm an actor. I work at the theater.

JOE Really? What are you doing now?

SUPER A love story. *(Romantic.)* I love you... I love you... I love you...

JOE Very good, Super Dog. Now, tell us. What do you do on Sunday?

SUPER On Sunday I correct homework.

JOE You correct homework? Why?

SUPER Well, in my free time, I'm an English teacher. Repeat after me, "I am, you are, he is, she is."

JOE Yes, thank you very much for coming to our program. Thank you.

SUPER My pleasure, Joe.

JOE *(To the audience.)* And now we're going to present...

SUPER It was a lot of fun.

JOE Yes, thank you very much.

SUPER Talking about my name.

JOE Yes, thank you.

SUPER And what I do.

JOE Yes, thank you. That's all. Thank you. *(To the audience.)* Now, we are going to...

SUPER I do other things, too.

JOE Yes.

SUPER I play soccer, tennis, basketball...

JOE Thank you. *(To the audience.)* And now...

SUPER *(Interrupting.)* I swim, run, dance, ride a bike...

JOE I said, thank you!

SUPER I travel a lot, I go to the movies...

JOE Bye! *(While Super Dog keeps on talking, Joe pushes him off of the stage. To the audience.)*[4] And now we're going to present the great rock group "The Puppies!"

(The Puppies enter.)

PUPPY 1 Hello, Joe.

PUPPY 2 Good evening!

PUPPY 3 It's good to be here, Joe!

JOE It's good to have you here.

PUPPY 4 We have a present for you, Joe.

JOE A present for me?

PUPPY 5 Yes. Here it is. *(Gives him a box of chocolates.)*

4. If you wish, you can end the sketch here, saying something like, "See you tomorrow."

JOE Oh, thank you, Puppies. I love chocolate. *(Opens it and starts eating it. Speaks with his mouth full.)* Hmm, it's delicious.

PUPPY 1 Can we talk about our new CD?

JOE No, let's talk about this delicious chocolate! Where did you buy it?

PUPPY 2 Well, we want to talk about our future shows...

JOE *(Still eating.)* Where can I buy more chocolate like this one?

PUPPY 3 Well, can we just give our telephone number in case somebody wants a show?

JOE Do you know the telephone number of the store where we can buy this chocolate?

PUPPY 4 *(Angry.)* No, we don't. *(To the other puppies.)* Well, puppies, let's sing!

PUPPY 5 Yeah. *(To the audience.)* The name of this song is...

JOE *(Interrupting.)* "The box of chocolates."

PUPPIES No!

PUPPY 1 It's called "Old McDonald Had a Dog Farm."[5]

PUPPY 2 Hit it, puppies!

(They sing, while Joe continues eating chocolate.)

PUPPIES *(Sing.)* Old McDonald had a dog farm
E-I-E-I-O
And on his farm he had a dog
E-I-E-I-O
With a bow-wow here and a bow-wow there
Here a bow-wow there a bow-wow
Everywhere a bow-wow
Old McDonald had a dog farm
E-I-E-I-O

Old McDonald had a dog farm
E-I-E-I-O
And on his farm he had two dogs
E-I-E-I-O

5. You can use any song here. It can be a song about dogs, or just a popular song at the moment.

With a bow-wow here and a bow-wow there
Here a bow-wow there a bow-wow
Everywhere a bow-wow
Old McDonald had a dog farm
E-I-E-I-O[6]

(At the end of the song.)

JOE Good bye, everybody. Thanks for watching "The Joe Puppy Program." See you tomorrow!

THE END

6. Sing the song many times, adding one dog at a time.

The Presidential Debate

LEVEL OF ENGLISH: Lower Intermediate

RECOMMENDED AGE: Any age. Students usually enjoy making fun of politicians. If you use the sketch with children, you might have to simplify the words a little bit.

STRUCTURES:

Grammar: Future with will
Vocabulary: Promises made by political candidates

NUMBER OF CHARACTERS: 9 – 3 journalists and 6 candidates. This number can be changed according to your need. You can have fewer or more journalists and candidates.

COSTUMES: The candidates can wear clothes that make them look like actual political candidates in your area. The journalists can wear clothes that make them look like TV personalities in your area.

PLAYING TIME: Between 6 and 10 minutes

SOME SUGGESTIONS:

- This is a good sketch to be used when you're having or have just had elections in your area. You can change the candidates to mayor or governor candidates.
- Although the candidates are numbers from a fictitious "Number World," you can change some of their lines to make them sound like real people that your students are familiar with.
- The candidates can sit or stand. Use the arrangement of a debate that has been seen on TV recently.

THE PRESIDENTIAL DEBATE

CHARACTERS	*Journalists 1 to 3* *Numbers 1 to 6*
JOURNALIST 1	Ladies and gentlemen. Next week we are going to elect the new president of Number World. This is the last debate with all the candidates. Let's hear what they have to say. Question number 1.
JOURNALIST 2	Number 1, why do you want to be the president of Number World?
NUMBER 1	Because I am the most important number of all.
JOURNALIST 3	What makes you so special?
NUMBER 1	Well, there is just one me.
NUMBER 2	One boring. Two is better than one.
NUMBER 1	Oh, yeah? Why?
NUMBER 2	Because everyone needs somebody. It's nicer to do things with someone.
NUMBER 6	You're wrong. Number six is the best number.
NUMBER 4	Oh, really? Don't make me laugh!
NUMBER 5	Number 5 is the best number.

(The numbers start shouting.)

JOURNALIST 1	Don't fight, please. Wait for your turn to speak.

(The numbers get quiet.)

JOURNALIST 2	So, Number 1, what are your plans for the government?
NUMBER 1	Well, we will have only *one* president, *one* vice-president, *one* governor for each state, *one* mayor for each city, *one* senate, and *one* house of representatives.
NUMBER 2	But we have that already.

NUMBER 1 *(Angry.)* Really? Who copied my idea?

(They all shout.)

JOURNALIST 3 Calm down, calm down, please. *(The numbers get quiet.)* Number 2, what are your plans?

NUMBER 2 Everybody will work *two* days a week only.

NUMBER 3 *(Angry.)* That's ridiculous. They won't have enough money.

NUMBER 2 Well, they could have *two* jobs.

JOURNALIST 1 Number 3. Is it true you are going to make a nuclear bomb?

NUMBER 3 *(Angry.)* No, it's not true. I'm going to make *three* nuclear bombs. My name is Number 3.

JOURNALIST 2 We know that.

NUMBER 3 *(Angry.)* Three things will be important in my government. Me, myself and I. My name is Number 3.

JOURNALIST 3 What about you, Number 4?

NUMBER 4 I will build a lot. I will make *four* tunnels. One tunnel from Brasília[1] to Salvador, one tunnel from Brasilia to São Paulo, one tunnel from Brasilia to Rio and one tunnel from Brasilia to Porto Alegre.[2]

JOURNALIST 1 Why tunnels? Isn't it easier to make roads?

NUMBER 4 I love tunnels. And roads and bridges...

JOURNALIST 2 Aren't they going to be expensive?

NUMBER 4 No, only *four* billion dollars... each. Don't forget: Number 4 is the number that does more.

JOURNALIST 3 Number 5, you said you want to create jobs. Is that true?

NUMBER 5 Yes! Everybody has the right to work. The present government is destroying our jobs. In my government I will create jobs for *five* million people, I will make *five* thousand schools, *five* hundred hospitals.

JOURNALIST 1 How are you going to do that?

NUMBER 5 *(Thinks.)* Uh... I don't know. But when I'm elected I will start thinking about it.

1. Use the name of the capital of your country.
2. Use names of cities in your country.

JOURNALIST 2 Number 6. You are the president of Number World. Why do you want to continue as president?

NUMBER 6 I did many good things. I reduced inflation to *six* percent a year.

NUMBER 5 Yeah, but many people lost their jobs.

NUMBER 4 And you didn't make any tunnels.

NUMBER 3 *(Angry.)* And you didn't make a nuclear bomb. And my name's Number 3.

NUMBER 1 I can't accept that. Each president should be elected only *one* time.

NUMBER 2 Well, *two* is a good number.

NUMBER 6 Well, to continue with the changes, I have to be elected *six* times.

NUMBER 3 *(Angry.)* Six times? Are you crazy? And my name is Number 3.

NUMBER 4 You don't do anything. Number 4 does more.

NUMBER 5 Let's fight!

(The numbers fight.)

JOURNALIST 3 Well, ladies and gentlemen, this is the end of our debate. Tomorrow we will have the debate among the candidates for governor, Numbers 7, 8, 9, 10, 11, and 12. See you tomorrow.

(Lights fade while the numbers are still fighting.)

THE END

The Rabbit Family Game – Version 1

LEVEL OF ENGLISH: Basic with very simple language

RECOMMENDED AGE: Children. You can use it with older and/or more advanced students if you make the questions more difficult and transform the characters into people.

STRUCTURES:

Grammar: Simple present, verb to be, yes or no questions
Vocabulary: Easter Vocabulary

NUMBER OF CHARACTERS: 8 – Two announcers and 6 rabbits. Rabbits 1 to 3 belong to Family 1. Rabbits 4 to 6 belong to Family 2. You can have more rabbits in each family if you prefer. Use one or two announcers to have the same number of contestants in each family. Change the names of the characters to suit your students' genders. See "The Rabbit Family Game – Version 2" for ideas of variations.

COSTUMES: The rabbits in the families can wear ordinary clothes and rabbit ears. They can have rabbit make up on, with whiskers and a pink nose. The announcers can wear more elegant clothes – a suit and tie for boys, a dress for girls. The announcers should have microphones. If they wear masks, choose half-masks that cover only the top of their heads – it's important for an actor to show his face, so he can show his emotions.

PLAYING TIME: Approximately 5 minutes

SOME SUGGESTIONS:

✷ You can use this play during Easter celebrations. You can create your own variations, using dogs, fairy tale characters, clowns, etc. Change the questions accordingly.
✷ You can use people instead of animals, and ask questions about a specific topic. For example, do "The New Zealand Game," and ask questions about New Zealand.
✷ The announcers stand in the center and each family stands at one side.
✷ At the end of the play they can all sing a song about Easter.

THE RABBIT FAMILY GAME – VERSION 1

CHARACTERS *Announcers 1 and 2*
Rabbits 1 to 6

ANNOUNCER 1 Welcome to the TV show "The Rabbit Family Game."

ANNOUNCER 2 A competition between two rabbit families.

ANNOUNCER 1 Here's family number one.

(Family 1 waves.)

RABBIT 1 Hello. I'm Peter Rabbit.

RABBIT 2 I'm Tim Rabbit.

RABBIT 3 My name is Joan Rabbit.

ANNOUNCER 2 And here is family number two.

(Family 2 waves.)

RABBIT 4 Hi. My name is Maria Rabbit.

RABBIT 5 I am Sue Rabbit.

RABBIT 6 Hello. My name is Mark Rabbit.

ANNOUNCER 1 Listen to the questions.

ANNOUNCER 2 You have three chances.

ANNOUNCER 1 Are you ready?

RABBITS Yes!

ANNOUNCER 2 Family one. It begins with C.

RABBIT 1 Is it a car?

ANNOUNCER 2 No, it isn't.

RABBIT 2 Is it a carrot?

ANNOUNCER 2 Yes, it is! Point to family one.

RABBITS 1, 2, 3 *(Jumping.)* Yes!

ANNOUNCER 1 Family two. It begins with E.

RABBIT 4 Is it an elephant?

ANNOUNCER 1 No, it isn't.

RABBIT 5 Is it an elevator?

ANNOUNCER 1 No, it isn't.

RABBIT 6 Is it an Easter egg?

ANNOUNCER 1 Yes, it is! Point to family two.

RABBITS 4, 5, 6 *(Jumping.)* Yes!

ANNOUNCER 2 Family one: What's this? *(Shows a picture of a basket with eggs.)*

RABBIT 3 Is it a box?

ANNOUNCER 2 No, it isn't.

RABBIT 1 Is it a jar?

ANNOUNCER 2 No, it isn't.

RABBIT 2 Is it a bag?

ANNOUNCER 2 No, it isn't. It's a basket. Sorry.

RABBITS 4, 5, 6 *(Jumping.)* Yes!

ANNOUNCER 1 Family two. Say *a* or *an*. Egg.

RABBIT 4 *An* egg.

ANNOUNCER 1 Very good. Point for family two.

RABBITS 4, 5, 6 *(Jumping.)* Yes!

ANNOUNCER 2 Family one. Say three things rabbits eat.

RABBIT 3 Leaves.

RABBIT 1 Carrots.

RABBIT 2 Grass.

ANNOUNCER 2 Very good! Point for family one!

RABBITS 1, 2, 3 *(Jumping.)* Yes!

ANNOUNCER 1 Two points for family one, two points for family two. Now family two. Say two things rabbits drink.

RABBIT 4 Water.

RABBIT 5 Orange juice.

ANNOUNCER 1 No! Rabbits don't drink orange juice. They drink milk.

RABBITS 1, 2, 3 *(Jumping.)* Yes!

RABBITS 4, 5, 6 Oh!

RABBIT 5 I'm sorry!

ANNOUNCER 2 Two points for family one, two points for family two. It's a tie. You are all winners.

ALL *(Jumping.)* Yeah!

ANNOUNCER 1 And now let's celebrate!

ALL *(Jumping.)* Yeah!

THE END

The Rabbit Family Game – Version 2

LEVEL OF ENGLISH: Basic

RECOMMENDED AGE: Children. You can use it with older and/or more advanced students if you make the questions more difficult and transform the characters into people.

STRUCTURES:

This play is a variation of the play "The Rabbit Family Game – Version 1," with more difficult structures and vocabulary.
Grammar: Simple present, verb to be, yes or no questions
Vocabulary: Easter Vocabulary

NUMBER OF CHARACTERS: 8 – 2 announcers and 6 rabbits. Rabbits 1 to 3 belong to Family 1. Rabbits 4 to 6 belong to Family 2. You can have more rabbits in each family if you prefer. Use one or two announcers to have the same number of contestants in each family. Change the names of the characters to suit your students' genders. See "The Rabbit Family Game – Version 1" for ideas of variations.

COSTUMES: The rabbits in the families can wear ordinary clothes and rabbit ears. They can have rabbit make up on, with whiskers and a pink nose. The announcers can wear more elegant clothes – a suit and tie for boys, a dress for girls. The announcers should have microphones. If they wear masks, choose half-masks that cover only the top of their heads – it's important for an actor to show his face, so he can show his emotions.

PLAYING TIME: Approximately 8 minutes

SOME SUGGESTIONS:

- The announcers stand in the center and each family stands at one side.
- You can use this play during Easter celebrations. You can create your own variations, using dogs, fairy tale characters, clowns, etc. Change the questions accordingly.
- You can use people instead of animals, and ask questions about a specific topic. For example, do "The Australia Game," and ask questions about Australia.
- At the end of the play they can all sing a song about Easter.

The Rabbit Family Game – Version 2

CHARACTERS *Announcers 1 and 2*
Rabbits 1 to 6

ANNOUNCER 1 Welcome to the TV show "The Rabbit Family Game."

ANNOUNCER 2 A competition between two rabbit families.

ANNOUNCER 1 Let's see which family knows more about rabbits.

ANNOUNCER 2 And here are the contestants of today's game.

ANNOUNCER 1 Here's family number one.

(Family 1 enters. They all wave.)

RABBIT 1 Hello, everybody.

RABBIT 2 It's good to be here.

RABBIT 3 We're very happy.

ANNOUNCER 2 Please introduce yourselves.

RABBIT 1 Hello. I'm Peter Rabbit.

RABBIT 2 I'm Tim Rabbit.

RABBIT 3 My name is Joan Rabbit.

ANNOUNCER 1 So, are you ready to play "The Rabbit Family Game?"

RABBIT 1 Yes, we are.

RABBIT 2 We're going to win.

RABBIT 3 We know everything about rabbits.

ANNOUNCER 2 Well, good luck. And here is family number two.

(Family 2 enters. They all wave.)

RABBIT 4 Good evening, everybody.

RABBIT 5 How are you?

RABBIT 6 Hello!

ANNOUNCER 1 Welcome to "The Rabbit Family Game."

RABBIT 4 Thank you very much.

RABBIT 5 We're very excited to be here.

ANNOUNCER 2 Do you know a lot about rabbits?

RABBIT 6 A lot? We know *everything* about rabbits!

RABBIT 4 We study a lot!

RABBIT 5 We are going to be the champions!

ANNOUNCER 1 Let's see. Please introduce yourselves.

RABBIT 4 Hi. My name is Maria Rabbit.

RABBIT 5 I am Sue Rabbit.

RABBIT 6 Hello. My name is Mark Rabbit.

ANNOUNCER 1 *(Shouts.)* Let's play "The Rabbit Family Game!" *(Everybody claps.)* Listen to the questions.

ANNOUNCER 2 You have three chances to answer.

ANNOUNCER 1 Are you ready to start?

ALL Yes!

ANNOUNCER 2 *(Shouts.)* So here we go! *(Everybody claps.)* Family one. It begins with C.

RABBIT 1 Is it a car?

ANNOUNCER 2 No, it isn't.

RABBIT 2 Is it a carrot?

ANNOUNCER 2 Yes, it is! Point for family one.

RABBITS 1, 2, 3 *(Jumping.)* Yes!

ANNOUNCER 2 Family one started well. What do you say, Family Two?

RABBIT 4 It's just beginner's luck.

ANNOUNCER 1 Family two. It begins with E.

RABBIT 4 Is it an elephant?

ANNOUNCER 1 No, it isn't.

RABBIT 5 Is it an elevator?

ANNOUNCER 1 No, it isn't.

RABBIT 6 Is it an Easter egg?

ANNOUNCER 1 Yes, it is! Point for family two.

RABBITS 4, 5, 6 *(Jumping.)* Yes!

ANNOUNCER 2 Family one. What's this? *(Shows a picture of a basket with eggs.)*

RABBIT 3 Is it a box?

ANNOUNCER 2 No, it isn't.

RABBIT 1 Is it a jar?

ANNOUNCER 2 No, it isn't.

RABBIT 2 Is it a bag?

ANNOUNCER 2 No, it isn't. It's a basket. Sorry.

RABBITS 4, 5, 6 *(Jumping.)* Yes!

ANNOUNCER 1 Family two. Say a or an. Egg.

RABBIT 4 An egg.

ANNOUNCER 1 Very good. Point for family two.

RABBITS 4, 5, 6 *(Jumping.)* Yes!

ANNOUNCER 2 Family one. Say three things rabbits eat.

RABBIT 3 That's easy. We eat leaves.

RABBIT 1 We eat carrots.

RABBIT 2 We eat grass.

ANNOUNCER 2 Very good! Point for family one!

RABBITS 1, 2, 3 *(Jumping.)* Yes!

ANNOUNCER 1 Two points for family one, two points for family two. Now family two. Say two things rabbits drink.

RABBIT 4 Water. We drink water!

RABBIT 5 And we drink orange juice.

ANNOUNCER 1 No! Rabbits don't drink orange juice. They drink milk.

RABBIT 6 *(To Rabbit 5.)* Orange juice? Are you crazy?

RABBIT 5 I'm sorry...

RABBITS 1, 2, 3 *(Jumping.)* Yes!

RABBITS 4, 5, 6 Oh!

ANNOUNCER 2 Two points for family one, two points for family two. It's a tie. You are all winners.

ALL *(Jumping.)* Yeah!

ANNOUNCER 2 And now let's celebrate! Everybody is going to get 10 bottles of Rabbit Cola, the best cola for rabbits.

ALL *(Jumping.)* Yeah!

ANNOUNCER 2 Good-bye, everybody and see you next week.

ALL *(Wave.)* Goodbye! Goodbye!

(They all celebrate.)

THE END

The Rich Old Man

LEVEL OF ENGLISH: Lower intermediate

RECOMMENDED AGE: Any age, but especially children (ages 8 and above) and teenagers.

STRUCTURES:

Grammar: Simple past and future with "will"
Vocabulary: Family relationships

NUMBER OF CHARACTERS: 15 – You can add other characters if you want to. The announcer and George can be played by the same actor.

COSTUMES: Get ideas from soap operas. Many of the characters are rich and the clothes have to be very exaggerated. The maid, the housekeeper, the nurse, the doctor and the priest have to dress according to their characters.

PLAYING TIME: Between 8 and 10 minutes

SOME SUGGESTIONS:

- This is a scene from a soap opera, so it has to be done in a very melodramatic way. The more students exaggerate, the funnier it will be.
- Mr. Rich can be sitting on a chair, with a blanket on his lap.
- You can ask students to write other sketches based on soap operas they watch on TV.

The Rich Old Man

CHARACTERS
Announcer
Mr. Rich
Rose, Mr. Rich's daughter
Joseph, Rose's husband
Daisy, Mr. Rich's daughter
George, Mr. Rich's son
Amanda, George's wife
Mildred, Mr. Rich's sister
Takatoshi, Mildred's husband
Ingrid, the housekeeper
Sally, the maid, Ingrid's daughter
Nancy, the secretary
Doctor
Priest
Nurse

ANNOUNCER Today is the day all of us have been waiting for: The last episode of the soap opera "The Rich Old Man." What will happen to the rich old man and his children? Who will get his money? Just watch and you will find out...

(We see the scene.)

MR. RICH *(On his death bed.)* Nurse! Nurse!

NURSE Did you call me, Mr. Rich?

MR. RICH Yes. I'm feeling very sick.

NURSE What's wrong?

MR. RICH I think I'm going to die. Please call my children.

NURSE OK. And I'll call the doctor and the priest, too.

(Rose, Daisy and Joseph enter.)

ROSE *(Pretending she's crying.)* Oh, Dad, oh, Dad. Are you really going to die?

DAISY *(Pushing Rose.)* Don't say that! You are fine, aren't you, Dad?

ROSE No, he isn't. He's very, very sick. Aren't you, Dad?

JOSEPH *(To Rose.)* Rose, stop that!

ROSE *(Whispers to Joseph.)* Oh, come on, Joseph. When he dies, I will get a lot of money. And half of it will be yours, because you are my husband.

JOSEPH *(Whispers to Rose.)* I know. But he's your father.

ROSE *(Whispers to Joseph.)* Yes. But he is not a good father. He only thinks about money. And now the money will be mine. *(Laughs.)*

SALLY *(Entering.)* Would you like some coffee?

DAISY Oh, yes, thank you.

SALLY *(Serving some coffee.)* How's Mr. Rich?

DAISY Not very well. It's just a question of days, maybe hours, maybe minutes.

SALLY Poor man... He's so kind...

(Ingrid enters.)

INGRID Excuse me, Mr. Rich. Mr. and Mrs. Takatoshi are here.

MR. RICH My sister and her husband!! What are they doing here? I haven't seen them for twenty years!

INGRID Please come in.

(Mildred and Takatoshi enter.)

MILDRED *(To Mr. Rich.)* Oh, my brother!

MR. RICH *(To Mildred.)* Oh, my sister!

TAKATOSHI *(To Mr. Rich.)* Oh, my brother-in-law!

MR. RICH *(To Takatoshi.)* Oh, my brother-in-law!

MILDRED Is it true? Are you dying?

MR. RICH Yes, I am. Oh, I'm so happy you are here. Now I can die in peace. I was very bad to you.

MILDRED Yes. You sent me away when I married Takatoshi.

TAKATOSHI Yes. Just because I was poor. But I've worked and worked, and now I have a lot of money.

MR. RICH Oh, I was so unfair!

TAKATOSHI Yes, you were. But let's forget it now.

MILDRED Yes, Richie, we are together now. And I want to spend the last minutes of your life with you.

SALLY *(Entering, bringing the doctor and the priest.)* Come in, please.

PRIEST *(To Daisy.)* Oh, I'm so sorry about your father. He was a good man.

MR. RICH I'm not dead yet!

PRIEST Sorry.

ROSE Don't worry. He'll die in a moment.

JOSEPH Rose!!

DOCTOR Open your mouth, Mr. Rich... *(Looks inside. Makes a very tragic face.)* There's nothing we can do now.

MR. RICH Doctor, I have to speak...

DOCTOR You can't speak. You have to rest.

MR. RICH No, I have to. But I need everybody here. Where's my son? Where's George?

(George runs in, followed by Amanda.)

GEORGE Daddy! Daddy! I came as soon as I heard.

DAISY Right. You are never here when we need you.

GEORGE Daddy. I have a surprise for you. I got married. This is my wife, Amanda.

AMANDA Nice to meet you, Mr. Rich.

PRIEST *(Recognizes her.)* Amanda!!

TAKATOSHI *(Recognizes her.)* Amanda!!

JOSEPH *(Recognizes her.)* Amanda!!

DOCTOR *(Recognizes her.)* Amanda!!

GEORGE Amanda, do you know these people?

AMANDA Uh... uh...

PRIEST So you got married, Amanda!

TAKATOSHI Oh, it's so good to see you again!

MILDRED *(Angry.)* Takatoshi, who's this woman?

DOCTOR *(To Amanda.)* You haven't changed a bit!

JOSEPH And you married my wife's brother! What a surprise!

GEORGE Stop that! What's going on here?

AMANDA Let me explain, George. I met them at the same place where I met you.

GEORGE At Super English School?[1]

AMANDA Yes. I was their teacher, too.

GEORGE What a coincidence!

MR. RICH Welcome to our family, Amanda. Now that everybody is here, I have something to say.

EVERYBODY What?

MR. RICH First, please call my secretary.

NANCY *(Enters.)* Did you call me, Mr. Rich?

TAKATOSHI Oh, she's very efficient...

MR. RICH Nancy, bring Ingrid and Sally.

NANCY Yes, Mr. Rich. *(Exits.)*

ROSE The maids? Why do you want the maids here?

MR. RICH Everybody has to hear what I have to say.

JOSEPH Oh, come on, Mr. Rich. We're very curious.

(Nancy, Ingrid and Sally enter.)

NANCY Here we are. Your housekeeper Ingrid and her daughter Sally.

MR. RICH The most important people in my life are here now. My daughter Daisy...

1. Use the name of your school.

DAISY *(Crying.)* Oh, Dad...

MR. RICH My daughter Rose...

ROSE *(Nasty.)* Come on, Dad. Say what you have to say.

MR. RICH My son-in-law Joseph...

JOSEPH You are like a father to me, Mr. Rich.

ROSE *(To Joseph.)* You are so false...

MR. RICH My dear son George...

GEORGE *(Crying.)* Daddy! Daddy!

MR. RICH My new daughter-in-law Amanda...

INGRID *(Recognizing her.)* Amanda!!

SALLY *(To Ingrid.)* Who is she, Mom?

INGRID She was my English teacher.

AMANDA Oh, this is so sad. I think I'm going to cry.

MR. RICH My sister Mildred...

MILDRED Finally we are together...

MR. RICH My brother-in-law Takatoshi...

TAKATOSHI Yes, I'm here.

MR. RICH And the real love of my life.

(All gasp.)

GEORGE The real love of your life? Who?

ROSE Your secretary! I knew it.

NANCY No, it isn't me. I'm married! I have five children.

MR. RICH No, it's... it's... argh! *(Feels sick.)*

DOCTOR Nurse?

NURSE Yes, doctor?

DOCTOR Give him a sedative.

NURSE All right, doctor.

MR. RICH No, no. I'm fine. I have to speak.

PRIEST Don't get too excited, my son.

MR. RICH When I was young and very poor, I married a woman. She was wonderful. But I wanted money. So I left her and married your mother, a very rich woman.

DAISY I can't believe it! You didn't love my mother?! You just wanted her money!

MR. RICH Yes, but I couldn't live without my first wife. So I decided to bring her to this house.

JOSEPH What? This is terrible!

MR. RICH Yes, I know, but I love her.

TAKATOSHI The suspense is killing me! Who is she?

INGRID *(Crying.)* Oh, this is too much for me. Come on, Richie, tell them.

GEORGE *(To Ingrid.)* So it's you!

SALLY Mother!

INGRID Yes, Sally. It's me. *(Points to Mr. Rich.)* And this is your father!

SALLY Mr. Rich is my father? *(Faints.)*

INGRID *(Trying to wake her up.)* Wake up, Sally. *(Sally wakes up.)* Yes, he is your father.

MR. RICH Yes, Sally. I'm your father. Sorry if I made you suffer. Come over here.

SALLY *(Runs to him, crying.)* Oh, Daddy! Oh, Daddy! Oh, Daddy!

ROSE The maid is my sister?

MR. RICH Yes, Rose. And I am going to leave all my money to her.

ROSE What?? You can't do that.

MR. RICH Yes, I can. You are all rich and Sally has nothing. I have to do this. I just want you to be friends. Argh! *(Dies.)*

DOCTOR *(Looks at him.)* He's dead.

(Everybody cries.)

ROSE Let's get out of here, Joseph. *(They exit.)*

DAISY *(Hugs Sally.)* Oh, Sally. We've been friends since we were children. I'm so happy to know that you are my sister.

MILDRED Well, this is a sad and a happy moment. But the family is together. That's the important thing.

NANCY What are you going to do now, Sally?

SALLY Oh, I don't know. I'll think about it tomorrow. After all, tomorrow is another day.[2]

(We hear the theme song from "Gone with the Wind.")

THE END

2. This is a famous line from the movie "Gone With the Wind."

The Scarecrows

LEVEL OF ENGLISH: Basic

RECOMMENDED AGE: Children, ages 8 and above

STRUCTURES:

Grammar: Simple present
Vocabulary: Parts of the body

NUMBER OF CHARACTERS: 15 – 8 scarecrows and Snow White's 7 dwarfs. You can change the number of scarecrows, but you have to keep the number of dwarfs. Dopey is a non-speaking character, but if you prefer you can have him say some lines.

COSTUMES: The scarecrows can wear jeans, checked shirts and straw hats. They can have a little straw showing from their sleeves. As for the seven dwarfs, get ideas from the movie and books.

PLAYING TIME: Between 8 and 10 minutes

SOME SUGGESTIONS:

✷ Have the scarecrows stand with their arms stretched. The ropes that tie them can be imaginary. When the dwarfs untie the scarecrows, they go behind them and pretend to be untying them.

The Scarecrows

CHARACTERS *Scarecrows 1 to 8*
Doc
Happy
Sleepy
Sneezy
Grumpy
Bashful
Dopey

(The scarecrows are standing on a field.)

SCARECROW 1 It's not easy to be a scarecrow.

SCARECROW 2 Yeah. And it's boring, too.

SCARECROW 3 All we do is stand here all day.

SCARECROW 4 It's "boo" here, and "boo" there.

SCARECROW 5 Everywhere a "boo, boo."

SCARECROW 6 I'm tired of this.

SCARECROW 7 Me too. My arms hurt.

SCARECROW 8 My legs hurt.

SCARECROW 1 My feet hurt.

SCARECROW 3 My shoulders hurt.

SCARECROW 4 My knees hurt.

SCARECROW 5 My head hurts.

SCARECROW 6 I ache all over.

SCARECROW 7 My body is stiff.

SCARECROW 8 So is mine.

SCARECROW 1 We have to get out of here.

SCARECROW 2 I agree. But how?

SCARECROW 3 I don't know.

SCARECROW 4 Me neither. Let's think.

SCARECROW 5 Listen, guys! Someone's coming.

SCARECROW 6 Maybe we can get some help.

SCARECROW 7 Yes. Maybe we will finally get out of here.

(The seven dwarfs come.)

DWARFS *(Sing.)* Hi-ho, hi-ho[1]
It's home from work we go
(They whistle.) Hi-ho, hi-ho, hi-ho, hi-ho

SLEEPY Hey, guys! Let's stop and rest. I'm tired. I want to sleep.

GRUMPY You're always tired. Come on! Let's go home!

SNEEZY *(Sneezes.)* Atchoo! Yes, let's go. This place makes me sneeze.

GRUMPY What do you mean by "this place makes me sneeze?" You're always sneezing.

HAPPY Come on, guys! Don't fight. Smile. Life is beautiful!

SCARECROW 8 Life is beautiful when you don't have to stand still all day.

DOC *(Looks around.)* Who said that?

SCARECROW 1 I didn't say anything.

SCARECROW 2 Me neither.

DOC *(To the scarecrows.)* Hey! Can you talk?

SCARECROW 3 Of course we can. Who do you think is talking?

SLEEPY Who are you?

SCARECROW 4 Who are *you*?

HAPPY I'm Happy.

DOC I'm Doc.

1. Use the song from the movie "Snow White and the Seven Dwarfs."

GRUMPY I'm Grumpy.

SNEEZY I'm... I'm... *(Sneezes.)* Atchoo... I'm Sneezy.

SLEEPY *(Yawns.)* I'm Sleepy.

SCARECROW 5 I can see that.

SCARECROW 6 *(To Bashful.)* Who are you?

BASHFUL *(Shy.)* I'm... I'm... I'm Bashful.

DOC *(Points to Dopey.)* And this is Dopey. He can't talk.

SCARECROW 7 Hey! I know who you are. You're the Seven Dwarfs, aren't you?

SCARECROW 8 You mean *the* Seven Dwarfs?

DWARFS Yes!

SCARECROW 1 I can't believe it! They're Snow White's Seven Dwarfs!

SCARECROW 2 Great! I know you're good men. Do you think you can help us?

HAPPY Sure! We're always glad to help.

DOC But what's the matter?

SCARECROW 3 We are tired of standing here day after day. We want to get out of here.

GRUMPY Oh-oh! I think *we* should get out of here.

SNEEZY No! Let's help these poor guys. Look! They can't move!

SCARECROW 4 Yes. Please help us!

DOC Don't worry. We're going to set you free.

(The Seven Dwarfs help set the scarecrows free.)

SCARECROWS *(Happy.)* Oh, wow!

SCARECROW 5 Oh, my! I'm free!

SCARECROW 6 Look! I can move, at last!

SCARECROWS We can all move!

SCARECROW 7 But I'm still a little stiff.

SCARECROW 8 Me too. We haven't exercised for a long time.

SCARECROW 1 Hey, guys! Move your heads.

(The scarecrows move their heads.)

SCARECROW 2 Move your shoulders.

(The scarecrows move their shoulders.)

SCARECROW 3 Move your knees.

(The scarecrows move their knees.)

SCARECROW 4 Hey! Why don't we do the head, shoulders, knees and toes dance?

SCARECROWS Great idea!

DOC What kind of dance is that?

SCARECROW 5 It's a dance that will help us exercise our joints.

SCARECROW 6 Let's do it now.

SCARECROW 7 It's fun.

GRUMPY I don't like to dance.

BASHFUL I can't dance. I'm too shy.

SLEEPY And I'm sleepy. I don't want to dance. I want to sleep. *(He yawns.)*

HAPPY Oh, come on, guys! It's going to be fun.

DWARFS OK.

SCARECROW 8 Is everybody ready? Here we go!

(They all sing and dance.)

ALL Head, shoulders, knees and toes[2]
Knees and toes

2. You can use other songs that mention body parts.

Head, shoulders, knees and toes
Knees and toes
And eyes and ears and mouth and nose
Oh, head, shoulders, knees and toes
Knees and toes

(The song ends.)

DOC Oh, that was nice!

SNEEZY *(Sneezes.)* Atchoo! Yes, I liked it.

HAPPY Well, guys, now we have to go.

SCARECROW 1 Hey! I have an idea. Can we go with you?

SCARECROW 2 Great idea! Can we?

SCARECROW 3 We can help you dig for diamonds.

SCARECROW 4 Yes! We're strong. And we won't eat your food. *(Shows the straw.)* Look! We are made of straw!

GRUMPY I don't know. We have to think about it.

DOC OK, guys. Let's talk.

(The dwarfs make a circle and talk.)

HAPPY Our answer is... Yes! You can come with us.

(The scarecrows jump happily.)

DOC So, what are we waiting for? Let's go!

ALL Yeah! Let's go.
(They exit, singing.) Hi-ho, hi-ho
It's home from work we go
(They whistle.) Hi-ho, hi-ho, hi-ho, hi-ho

THE END

The Secret

LEVEL OF ENGLISH: Basic, with very simple language

RECOMMENDED AGE: Children, ages 5 to 12

STRUCTURES:

Grammar: Simple present, very basic
Vocabulary: Parts of the body

NUMBER OF CHARACTERS: 13 people – You can have as many people as you want. We need at least 3 people. One to tell the secret, one to tell it to somebody else, and a third one to hear it.

COSTUMES: Ordinary clothes

PLAYING TIME: Approximately 3 minutes

SOME SUGGESTIONS:

- You don't need any special setting to present this sketch.
- When each character hears the secret, they have to react in a very exaggerated way, showing that it's really unbelievable. The more the actors exaggerate, the funnier it will be.
- You can adapt this sketch and have different secrets, such as numbers from 1 to 10, the days of the week, the months of the year, the alphabet and many others.
- If your students can't read yet, teach them one line at a time. Then have them repeat the whole sketch from the beginning (or as we say in theater, "from the top.")

The Secret

CHARACTERS *People 1 to 13*

(Person 1 is on stage. Person 2 enters.)

PERSON 1 Hi!

PERSON 2 Hello. Do you want to know a secret?

PERSON 1 A secret? Yes, I love secrets.

PERSON 2 Do you promise not to tell anybody?

PERSON 1 Of course, I do. Tell me.

PERSON 2 What?

PERSON 1 The secret!

PERSON 2 The secret? *(After a pause.)* Sorry, I can't.

PERSON 1 Why not?

PERSON 2 It's a secret.

PERSON 1 Oh, come on. Tell me! I won't tell anybody.

PERSON 2 OK. Here we go. *(Whispers.)* Head, shoulders, knees and toes.

PERSON 1 *(Very surprised.)* Knees and toes?

PERSON 2 *(Whispers.)* Head, shoulders, knees and toes.

PERSON 1 *(Very surprised.)* Knees and toes?

PERSON 2 *(Whispers.)* And eyes, and ears, and mouth and nose.

PERSON 1 *(Very surprised.)* Oh, my God!

PERSON 2 *(Whispers.)* Head, shoulders, knees and toes.

PERSON 1 *(Very surprised.)* Knees and toes?

PERSON 2 I have to go now. Promise you won't tell anybody.

PERSON 1 I promise.

PERSON 2 Good bye! *(Exits.)*

(A group of people enters.)

PERSON 1 Hey, guys, do you want to know a secret?

PERSON 3 Yes.

PERSON 4 Sure.

PERSON 5 Of course.

PERSON 6 I love secrets.

PERSON 1 Gather round.

(They all get in a circle around Person 1, putting their arms around each other's shoulders. Person 1 whispers. When each person speaks, they raise their heads so that we see them sticking out of the group.)

PERSON 1 *(Whispers very softly so that the audience doesn't hear.)* Head, shoulders, knees and toes.

PERSON 7 Oh, my God!

PERSON 1 *(Whispers very softly so that the audience doesn't hear.)* Knees and toes.

PERSON 8 Really?

PERSON 1 *(Whispers very softly so that the audience doesn't hear.)* Head, shoulders, knees and toes.

PERSON 9 I can't believe it!

PERSON 1 *(Whispers very softly so that the audience doesn't hear.)* Knees and toes.

PERSON 10 That's incredible!

PERSON 1 *(Whispers very softly so that the audience doesn't hear.)* And eyes and ears and mouth and nose.

PERSON 11 That's surprising!

PERSON 1 *(Whispers very softly so that the audience doesn't hear.)* Head, shoulders, knees and toes.

PERSON 12 That's amazing!

PERSON 1 *(Whispers very softly so that the audience doesn't hear.)* Knees and toes.

PERSON 13 My Goodness!

(They undo the circle.)

PERSON 1 Did you understand?

PERSON 12 Yes, we did.

PERSON 1 So here we go!

(They all sing and dance.)

ALL Head, shoulders, knees and toes
Knees and toes
Head, shoulders, knees and toes
Knees and toes
And eyes and ears and mouth and nose
Oh, head, shoulders, knees and toes
Knees and toes

(They all bow and exit. Person 2 enters.)

PERSON 2 *(Annoyed, to the audience.)* Some people can't keep a secret...

THE END

THE TRAFFIC JAM

LEVEL OF ENGLISH: Basic, with very simple lines

RECOMMENDED AGE: Children, ages 6 to 10

STRUCTURES:

Grammar: Simple present and simple future
Vocabulary: very simple

NUMBER OF CHARACTERS: 12 drivers. You can add or eliminate some drivers.

COSTUMES: Ordinary clothes

PLAYING TIME: Approximately 3 minutes plus the song

SOME SUGGESTIONS:

✸ Each character is inside his/her car, in a traffic jam. To represent this, they should all hold a steering wheel (they can make one) and stand in line facing the side wall. Before each character speaks, he/she puts his/her head out of the car window. The others look.
✸ Choose a popular song that will make students dance a lot.
✸ When they sing and dance, they get out of the line and move around the stage. When the song ends, they have to be in line again.

The Traffic Jam

CHARACTERS *Drivers 1 to 12*

(The drivers enter, driving their cars. Then they all stop.)

DRIVER 1 This traffic is terrible.

DRIVER 2 It sure is. Really bad.

DRIVER 3 I'm in a hurry. I want to go home.

DRIVER 4 Me too, but what can we do?

DRIVER 5 Nothing. We have to wait.

DRIVER 6 What happened?

DRIVER 7 An accident, maybe.

DRIVER 8 I don't think so.

DRIVER 9 It's just rush hour.

DRIVER 10 Every day it's the same thing.

DRIVER 11 I'm tired of this.

DRIVER 12 So am I.

DRIVER 1 *(Honking.)* Come on! Move!

DRIVER 2 *(To Driver 1.)* Stop honking!

DRIVER 3 Yes, stop it.

DRIVER 4 You won't make the cars move.

DRIVER 5 It will just make the place noisier.

DRIVER 6 And people more nervous.

DRIVER 7 I'm already nervous.

DRIVER 8 Me too. I need to relax.

DRIVER 9 Hey, I have an idea!

DRIVER 10 What is it?

DRIVER 9 Let's listen to music.

DRIVER 11 Listen to music? Are you crazy?

DRIVER 9 And let's dance, too.

DRIVER 12 Yes, this will make time pass faster.

DRIVER 1 Hey everybody, turn on your radios!

DRIVER 2 Let's dance!

(They turn on their radios. They sing and dance. While they sing and dance, they honk their horns a lot. When the song ends they continue talking.)

DRIVER 3 *(Pointing.)* Hey, look! The cars are moving!

DRIVER 4 Yeah, let's go home! Finally!

DRIVER 5 That was fun.

DRIVER 6 It really helped us to relax.

DRIVER 7 Maybe we can do it again tomorrow.

DRIVER 8 Good idea! Let's meet again here.

DRIVER 10 At the same time, OK?

DRIVER 11 OK, guys, see you tomorrow.

DRIVER 12 See you...

DRIVER 9 And don't forget your horns.

(The cars move. They all exit.)

THE END

THE UNDER THE SEA HOSPITAL

LEVEL OF ENGLISH: Basic

RECOMMENDED AGE: Children (ages 8 and above) and teenagers

STRUCTURES:

Grammar: Simple present and present perfect
Vocabulary: Ailments

NUMBER OF CHARACTERS: 8 – a doctor, a receptionist and 6 patients. You can add more patients, by dividing the lines and/or writing other lines. You can create other ailments for the other patients.

COSTUMES: The actors can wear very colorful clothes to represent the fish. They can also wear masks. However, the masks should not cover all their faces or the audience won't be able to see their facial expressions. They can cover only the eyes or they can be worn on top of their heads.

PLAYING TIME: Approximately 10 minutes

SOME SUGGESTIONS:

✷ Although the action takes place under the sea, the setting can look like a real public hospital. Use a desk for the receptionist and some chairs for the patients in the waiting room.

The Under the Sea Hospital

CHARACTERS	*Receptionist* *Doctor* *Patients 1 to 6*

(A public hospital under the sea. The patients are waiting in the waiting room. Patient 1 enters.)

PATIENT 1 Excuse me...

RECEPTIONIST Yes? Can I help you?

PATIENT 1 I need to see a doctor.

RECEPTIONIST You need a sea doctor? Then you're in the right place. The Under the Sea Hospital.

PATIENT 1 No, no, no. I need to see a doctor.

RECEPTIONIST Oh, I understand. OK. Sit down and wait.

PATIENT 1 Wait? But this is an emergency!

RECEPTIONIST I'm sorry. All these fish are waiting. You're next.

PATIENT 1 How long do I have to wait?

RECEPTIONIST Not too long. Here's a card with a number. Wait until we call you. *(Gives him a card.)*

PATIENT 1 *(Reading.)* Four hundred and fifty-eight. *(To the audience.)* Oh, my Neptune![1]

RECEPTIONIST *(Calling.)* Number 27, please!

PATIENT 1 Twenty-seven?

PATIENT 2 *(Happy.)* That's me! Finally! I've been waiting for seven hours!

PATIENT 3 Seven hours?

PATIENT 4 Well, I've been waiting for five hours.

1. This is equivalent to "Oh, my God!" since Neptune is the god of the seas.

PATIENT 5 Oh, my Neptune!

RECEPTIONIST *(To Patient 2.)* What's your name?

PATIENT 2 Willy.

RECEPTIONIST *(Writing down.)* What's your last name?

PATIENT 2 Last name? I don't have a last name!

RECEPTIONIST You don't have a last name?

PATIENT 2 No. Fish don't have last names!

RECEPTIONIST Oh, yes. I forgot... What kind of fish are you?

PATIENT 2 I'm a tuna fish.

RECEPTIONIST Where do you live?

PATIENT 2 In the sea.

RECEPTIONIST OK. Sit down and wait.

PATIENT 2 Wait? Where is the doctor?

RECEPTIONIST Just sit down and wait.

PATIENT 6 It's not easy to find a doctor in this hospital.

PATIENT 4 That's true.

PATIENT 5 Public hospitals under the sea are really bad.

PATIENT 6 I'm tired of waiting. I'm really sick.

PATIENT 3 What's your problem?

PATIENT 6 I ate a piece of plastic.

PATIENT 4 Oh, my Neptune!

PATIENT 5 You have to watch what you eat!

PATIENT 1 Yes. Humans throw garbage in the sea and cause us many problems.

PATIENT 6 I know. I have a terrible stomachache. I can't swim!

PATIENT 2 Don't worry. The doctor will give you some medicine.

PATIENT 5 You'll be fine soon.

PATIENT 6 I hope so.

(The doctor enters.)

DOCTOR *(To the receptionist.)* Good afternoon.

RECEPTIONIST Good afternoon, doctor.

DOCTOR You can call the next patient, please.

RECEPTIONIST OK, doctor. *(Calling.)* Number 45.

PATIENT 4 That's me!

PATIENT 5 Forty-five? You're not calling the numbers in order!

RECEPTIONIST I know. It's very difficult to keep the cards in order under the water. They float and then we don't know the order anymore.

PATIENT 6 *(To the audience.)* It's not easy to live under the sea.

DOCTOR *(To Patient 4.)* Open your mouth. *(Patient 4 opens her mouth.)* Say, "Ahhhh!"

PATIENT 4 Ahhh!

DOCTOR Take this medicine and you'll feel better. *(Gives Patient 4 a box.)*

PATIENT 4 But I have a backache.

DOCTOR No problem. This medicine is good for everything.

PATIENT 4 Are you sure?

RECEPTIONIST *(To Patient 4.)* Please go now, because there are many people waiting.

PATIENT 4 OK.

DOCTOR Who's next?

RECEPTIONIST *(Calling.)* Number six hundred and ninety-nine!

PATIENT 3 Here! *(Stands up and walks toward the doctor.)* Finally! I'm tired...

DOCTOR You're tired?

PATIENT 3 Yes.

DOCTOR Take this medicine and you'll feel better. *(Gives Patient 3 a box.)*

PATIENT 3 But I'm tired of waiting.

DOCTOR That's OK. You'll be fine anyway. This medicine is really great!

PATIENT 3 But what about my problem?

DOCTOR One problem at a time, only.

RECEPTIONIST If you want to have another problem, get another card and wait again.

PATIENT 3 This is not a very good hospital.

DOCTOR Yes, it is. It's the best public hospital under the sea.

PATIENT 5 No, it isn't

RECEPTIONIST Yes, it is. It's really wonderful.

PATIENT 6 What's so good about it?

DOCTOR Well, it's full of patients.

PATIENT 5 So what?

DOCTOR If many patients come here, it means it's a good hospital.

PATIENT 5 No, it doesn't. You don't give the patients the right treatment.

PATIENT 6 That's right.

PATIENT 3 The doctors are very bad here.

DOCTOR No, they're not.

PATIENTS Yes, they are.

PATIENT 4 This hospital is dirty. It smells bad.

RECEPTIONIST We're under the sea. It smells like fish!

DOCTOR Look, everybody. You're all very angry. Relax. *(Shows a box.)* Take this medicine and you'll feel better.

PATIENT 1 You only give the same medicine.

PATIENT 2 What kind of doctor are you?

DOCTOR I'm a fish-oh-therapist.

RECEPTIONIST He's the best doctor under the sea.

PATIENT 3 If he's the best, I don't want to meet the worst.

(We hear a bell.)

PATIENT 6 What's that?

RECEPTIONIST It's six o'clock. Time to close the hospital.

PATIENT 4 What?

PATIENT 5 But we are sick!

PATIENT 6 You can't close it now!

RECEPTIONIST Yes, I can. The doctor has to leave.

DOCTOR I'm sorry, but I have to go. I have a doctor's appointment.

PATIENT 5 Why don't you see a doctor here?

DOCTOR Are you crazy? In this hospital? No way... *(Exits.)*

PATIENT 4 Public hospitals are really bad.

PATIENT 3 On land and in the sea...

THE END

THE WHEELS ON THE BUS

LEVEL OF ENGLISH: Basic, with very simple language

RECOMMENDED AGE: Children, ages 5 to 8

STRUCTURES:

Grammar: Simple present
Vocabulary: The bus, parts of the bus

NUMBER OF CHARACTERS: 6 – A teacher and 5 students. You can add more students if you want to. The teacher has the most difficult lines. The students' lines are very simple.

COSTUMES: The teacher can wear clothes that make him/her look older. Children can borrow clothes from their parents or grandparents. The students can wear a uniform; for example, blue shorts or skirt and a white T-shirt.

PLAYING TIME: Between 3 and 5 minutes

SOME SUGGESTIONS:

✱ Place a sign with the words "Bus Stop" on the wall or on a stand. The teacher and the students stand next to it.
✱ If your students can't read yet, teach them one line at a time. Then have them repeat the whole sketch from the beginning (or as we say in theater, "from the top.")

The Wheels on the Bus

CHARACTERS *Teacher*
Students 1 to 5

(The teacher and the students approach a bus stop.)

TEACHER OK, is everybody here?

STUDENTS Yes!

TEACHER Good. Today we are here to learn more things about our city.

STUDENT 1 Great!

TEACHER What did we study in our class yesterday?

CHILDREN The bus!

TEACHER Right! *(Points to the bus stop.)* What's this?

STUDENT 2 I don't know.

STUDENT 3 It's a bus stop.

TEACHER Very good. It's a bus stop! What do people do at a bus stop?

STUDENTS They wait for the bus!

TEACHER Very good! They wait for the bus. You are good students.

STUDENT 4 Of course.

STUDENT 5 We study at Super English School.[1]

TEACHER What do you know about the bus?

STUDENT 1 It's big.

STUDENT 2 It has four wheels.

STUDENT 3 It takes people to many places.

1. Use the name of your school.

STUDENT 4 The bus driver drives the bus.

STUDENT 5 You have to pay to take the bus.

TEACHER Very good. You're very good students.

STUDENT 1 You're a very good teacher.

STUDENTS Yes!

TEACHER Thank you.

STUDENT 2 And Super English School is a good school!

STUDENTS Yes!

TEACHER Thanks. Let's see if you remember what we studied. How do the wheels on the bus go?

STUDENTS The wheels on the bus go round and round.

TEACHER How do the people on the bus go?

STUDENTS The people on the bus go up and down.

TEACHER How does the horn on the bus go?

STUDENTS The horn on the bus goes too, too, too.

TEACHER How does the money on the bus go?

STUDENTS The money in the bus goes ding, ding, ding.

TEACHER How does the wiper on the glass go?

STUDENTS The wiper on the glass goes sweesh, sweesh, sweesh.

TEACHER How do the doors on the bus go?

STUDENTS The doors on the bus go open and shut.

TEACHER What does the driver on the bus say?

STUDENTS The driver on the bus says, "Move on back."

TEACHER Very good! You're excellent students! Now let's sing and dance!

(They all sing and dance.)

ALL The wheels on the bus go round and round

Round and round, round and round
The wheels on the bus go round and round
All through the town

The people on the bus go up and down
Up and down, up and down
The people on the bus go up and down
All through the town

The horn on the bus goes too, too, too
Too, too, too, too, too, too
The horn on the bus goes too, too, too
All through the town

The money in the bus goes ding, ding, ding
Ding, ding, ding, ding, ding, ding
The money in the bus goes ding, ding, ding
All through the town

The wiper on the glass goes sweesh, sweesh, sweesh
Sweesh, sweesh, sweesh, sweesh, sweesh, sweesh
The wiper on the glass goes sweesh, sweesh, sweesh
All through the town

The doors on the bus go open and shut
Open and shut, open and shut
The doors on the bus go open and shut
All through the town

The driver on the bus says, "Move on back"
Move on back, move on back
The driver on the bus says, "Move on back"
All through the town

THE END

Think of Your Fingers

LEVEL OF ENGLISH: Basic

RECOMMENDED AGE: Any age. If you use this sketch with teenagers and adults you can make the lines a little bit more advanced.

STRUCTURES:

Grammar: Simple present, imperative
Vocabulary: Ailments and solutions, numbers from 1 to 5

NUMBER OF CHARACTERS: 7 – a doctor, a nurse and 5 patients. You can have other nurses, too. Just divide the lines accordingly. However, the number of patients can't be changed, because the sketch is all about the number five.
If you have more actors, you can have 10 patients in line and then count the fingers on both hands.

COSTUMES: The doctor can wear white clothes. The nurse can wear white clothes and a nurse's hat. The patients can wear ordinary clothes that show how they feel. For example, the person who's hoarse can have a scarf around his neck.

PLAYING TIME: Between 4 and 6 minutes

SOME SUGGESTIONS:

✸ Divide the space you have into two parts: the doctor's office and the waiting room. In the doctor's office you need a chair and a desk. In the waiting room you can just have an empty space where the people stand in line or you can have five chairs. Each time one patient enters the doctor's office, the other patients move to the next chair.

Think of Your Fingers

CHARACTERS *Nurse*
Doctor
Patients 1 to 5

(At a public hospital. A lot of sick people are waiting in line. The doctor is sitting. The doctor looks at the nurse and shows the number 1 with his finger.)

NURSE *(To the patients in line.)* Patient number one, please.

PATIENT 1 That's me.

NURSE You can come in.

PATIENT 1 *(Enters.)* Thank you.

DOCTOR What's the matter?

PATIENT 1 Well, doctor, I have a headache.

DOCTOR No problem. Just take five aspirins.

PATIENT 1 Five aspirins? How many is that?

DOCTOR Five! Like your fingers! *(Shows his fingers and counts.)* One, two, three, four, five.[1]

PATIENT 1 Oh, yes! My fingers! *(Counts.)* 1-2-3-4-5. Thank you, Doctor. *(Exits.)*

(The doctor looks at the nurse and shows the number 2 with his fingers.)

NURSE *(To the people in line.)* Patient number 2, please.

PATIENT 2 *(Hoarse.)* Here.

NURSE The doctor is waiting.

PATIENT 2 *(Hoarse.)* Thank you. *(Enters.)*

DOCTOR Hello.

1. The doctor can sing instead of counting. Use any familiar tune, like "Happy Birthday to You."

PATIENT 2 *(Hoarse.)* Hello.

DOCTOR What's the matter with you?

PATIENT 2 *(Hoarse.)* Oh, doctor, I lost my voice.

DOCTOR No problem. Just drink five cups of lemon tea.

PATIENT 2 Five cups? How many is that?

DOCTOR Just think of your fingers. *(Counts showing the fingers.)* It's one, two, three, four, five.

PATIENT 2 *(Happy.)* Thanks very much, doctor. Bye. *(Exits.)*

(The doctor looks at the nurse and shows the number 3 with his fingers.)

NURSE *(To the people in line.)* Patient number 3.

PATIENT 3 Yes, here I am.

NURSE It's your turn. Come in, please.

PATIENT 3 Thank you, nurse. *(Enters.)* Hello, doctor.

DOCTOR Sit down, please. *(The patient sits.)* Now, what's your problem?

PATIENT 3 Well, doctor, I have five children. Every morning I take my children to school, but I always leave one at home.

DOCTOR Really? Why?

PATIENT 3 Well, I don't know. I always count them, but I guess I have a problem with the number five.

DOCTOR Well, the solution is very easy.

PATIENT 3 Is it, doctor?

DOCTOR All you have to do is think of your fingers *(Counts showing the fingers.)* One, two, three, four, five.

PATIENT 3 That's a great idea, doctor. You are wonderful. Thank you. *(Exits.)*

(The doctor looks at the nurse and shows the number 4 with his fingers.)

NURSE *(To the people in line.)* Patient number four. You can come in now. The doctor is waiting.

PATIENT 4 Thanks, nurse. *(Enters.)*

DOCTOR Good morning.

PATIENT 4 Good morning, doctor.

DOCTOR What can I do for you?

PATIENT 4 You know, doctor. I want to go on a diet. I have to lose five kilos, but I never remember how much five is.

DOCTOR You came to the right doctor.

PATIENT 4 Really? Why?

DOCTOR I can help you.

PATIENT 4 How?

DOCTOR Just think of your fingers. *(Counts showing the fingers.)* One, two, three, four, five.

PATIENT 4 Thanks, doctor. That's great! *(Exits.)*

(The doctor doesn't move.)

NURSE *(To the doctor.)* Who's the next patient, doctor?

DOCTOR Well, let me see. *(Thinks.)* I saw Patient 1, Patient 2, Patient 3 and Patient 4. So now I have to see patient... *(Thinks.)* Oh, I don't remember!

PATIENT 5 *(Entering.)* Come on, doctor, that's very easy.

DOCTOR Really?

PATIENT 5 Yes. All you have to do is... *(Counts showing the fingers.)* One, two, three, four, five. Just think of your fingers.

DOCTOR Oh, you're right! Patient 5 is the next patient.

PATIENT 5 That's me. May I come in?

DOCTOR *(Looking at his watch.)* Sorry. It's five o'clock. It's time for me to go. Come back in five days. *(Exits.)*

THE END

This Is Your Face

LEVEL OF ENGLISH: Basic

RECOMMENDED AGE: Children, ages 7 to 12

STRUCTURES:

Grammar: Simple present
Vocabulary: Parts of the body and actions related to them

NUMBER OF CHARACTERS: 15 – The host and 14 audience members. You can have as many people in the audience as you want. Just distribute the line accordingly. You can also include more questions. When there's no number after the word "Audience," all the members of the audience speak together.

COSTUMES: Ordinary clothes for the audience members. Fancy clothes for the host. The host can also wear very funny clothes, with a funny hat or funny glasses.

PLAYING TIME: Between 6 and 8 minutes

SOME SUGGESTIONS:

* Put two rows of chairs on each side of the stage, for the audience members to sit. They could also sit on the floor.
* The host can stand in the center and move to the audience when he talks to them.
* When the host selects a person to answer a question, this person can go to the center with him.
* The host can have a stage assistant to hold the box with pieces of paper. She doesn't have to say anything. Just stand there with a big smile, just like on some TV shows. The assistant could also be the one who reads the questions from the cards.
* At the end you can sing any song that mentions the face or parts of the face.

This Is Your Face

CHARACTERS *Host*
Audience 1 to 14

HOST Welcome to the TV show "This is Your Face!" *(Everybody cheers.)* This is a TV show dedicated to that wonderful body part – the face.

AUDIENCE *(Shouting.)* Face! Face! Face! Yeah...

HOST Today we have many people in the audience! *(Everybody cheers.)* Let's talk to some of them.

(The host gets near the audience and gives some people the microphone.)

AUDIENCE 1 Hi, I love my face!

AUDIENCE 2 Hello. I love all the faces!

AUDIENCE *(Shouting.)* Face! Face! Face! Yeah...

AUDIENCE 3 *(Excited.)* Hello, Mommy. Look at my face on TV!

AUDIENCE 4 Faces are wonderful!

AUDIENCE 5 Faces are great!

AUDIENCE *(Shouting.)* Face! Face! Face! Yeah...

HOST As you can see, everybody is excited here today. *(Everybody cheers.)* And now we're going to select our first contestant. *(To the audience.)* Do you all have your numbers?

AUDIENCE *(Showing pieces of paper.)* Yes!

HOST So, pay attention. *(Gets a box full of pieces of paper and draws one.)* The first contestant is number 73.

AUDIENCE 6 *(Jumping, happy.)* It's me! It's me! *(Goes to the front.)*

HOST Welcome to the show.

AUDIENCE 6 Thank you. I'm a big fan! I'm very happy to be here.

HOST Good. So here's your question. Listen and tell me the part of the face. *(Reads.)* "We are a part of the face. Sometimes we're brown, black, blue or green. We are very nice and you use us to see with. What are we?"

AUDIENCE 6 *(Thinks for a while.)* The eyes?

HOST That's correct!

AUDIENCE 6 *(Jumps, happy.)* Yes! Yes! Yes!

(The audience claps.)

HOST Here's 100 dollars. Would you like to stop or would you like to continue?

AUDIENCE *(Shouts.)* Continue! Continue!

AUDIENCE 7 Stop! Stop!

AUDIENCE 8 Continue! Continue!

AUDIENCE 6 I'll continue.

(Everybody claps. Audience 7 frowns.)

HOST OK, we're going to continue to talk about eyes.

AUDIENCE 6 OK.

HOST How many eyes does a person have?

AUDIENCE Oh...

AUDIENCE 9 That's too easy!

HOST *(To the audience.)* Silence please. *(To Audience 6.)* So, how many eyes does a person have?

AUDIENCE 6 Two?

HOST *(Shouts.)* That is correct! *(The audience claps.)* You got 100 dollars more.

AUDIENCE 6 *(Jumps, happy.)* Yes! Yes! Yes!

HOST Would you like to stop or would you like to continue?

AUDIENCE *(Shouts.)* Continue! Continue!

AUDIENCE 7 Stop! Stop!

AUDIENCE 8 Continue! Continue!

AUDIENCE 6 I'll stop.

AUDIENCE Oh...

(Audience 7 claps.)

HOST We're going to select another contestant. *(To the audience.)* Do you all have your numbers?

AUDIENCE *(Showing pieces of paper.)* Yes!

HOST So, pay attention. *(Gets a box full of pieces of paper and draws one.)* The second contestant is number 534.

AUDIENCE 10 *(Jumps, happy.)* Me! Me! Me!

HOST Come here please!

AUDIENCE 10 *(Going onstage.)* I can't believe I was selected. I love this program!

HOST Thank you. Now are you ready for your question?

AUDIENCE 10 Yes, I'm ready!

HOST *(Reads.)* "One eye here and one eye there. A mouth at the bottom and one ear at each side. Top everything with some hair. What's in the middle?"

AUDIENCE *(Whispering.)* Nose... Nose...

HOST *(To the audience.)* Please don't help the contestant. Keep quiet. *(To Audience 10.)* So what's the answer?

AUDIENCE 10 Can you repeat the question?

HOST Yes, of course. *(Reads.)* "One eye here and one eye there. A mouth at the bottom and one ear at each side. Top everything with some hair. What's in the middle?"

AUDIENCE *(Whispering.)* Nose... Nose...

HOST *(To the audience.)* Silence, please.

AUDIENCE 10 I know! It's the nose!

HOST I'm sorry. The audience helped you. You can't get the prize.

AUDIENCE 10 *(Angry, shouts at the audience.)* Why did you help me? I knew the answer!

AUDIENCE Boo... Boo...

HOST Let's select another contestant. *(To the audience.)* Do you all have your numbers?

AUDIENCE *(Showing pieces of paper.)* Yes!

HOST All right then, pay attention. *(Gets a box full of pieces of paper and draws one.)* The next contestant is number 1.

AUDIENCE 11 *(Jumps, happy.)* Me! Me! Me!

HOST Congratulations! Are you ready?

AUDIENCE 11 Yes, I'm ready! Of course!

HOST I'm going to say some words and you have to show them with your face. OK?

AUDIENCE 11 Only with my face?

HOST Of course. This is the TV program *(Shouts.)* "*This is your Face!*"

(Everybody cheers.)

AUDIENCE *(Shouting.)* Face! Face! Face! Yeah...

AUDIENCE 11 Oh, yes...

HOST So here we go! Happy. *(Audience 11 makes a happy face.)* Sad. *(Audience 11 makes a sad face.)* Angry. *(Audience 11 makes an angry face.)* Really mad. *(Audience 11 makes a really mad face.)* Congratulations! You got 400 dollars.

AUDIENCE 11 *(Very happy.)* Wow!

HOST Look at your face! Now you look really happy.

AUDIENCE 11 Yes, I am!

HOST And now it's time for the "What can you do?" questions. *(Everybody cheers.)* You get 10 dollars for each correct answer. Who wants to answer a question?

AUDIENCE *(Raise their hands and shout.)* Me! Me! Me!

HOST *(To Audience 12.)* What do you do with your eyes?

AUDIENCE 12 I see with my eyes.

HOST Right! Here's 10 dollars. *(Gives 10 dollars to Audience 12.)*

AUDIENCE *(Raise their hands and shout.)* Me! Me! Me!

HOST *(To Audience 13.)* What do you do with your nose?

AUDIENCE 13 I smell with my nose.

HOST Right! Here's 10 dollars. *(Gives 10 dollars to Audience 13.)*

AUDIENCE *(Raise their hands and shout.)* Me! Me! Me!

HOST *(To Audience 14.)* What do you do with your chin?

AUDIENCE 14 With my chin? *(Points to his chin.)*

HOST Yes. What do you do with your chin?

AUDIENCE 14 I don't know.

HOST *(Shouts.)* That's the correct answer! Nobody knows what a chin can do. Here's 10 dollars.

AUDIENCE 14 *(Happy.)* I can't believe it!

(The audience claps.)

HOST Well, everybody, that's all the time we have. It's time to say goodbye.

AUDIENCE Oh...

HOST We'll be back tomorrow with another edition of "This is your Face!" *(Everybody cheers.)* But before we go, let's sing together. *(Everybody cheers.)* Let's sing a song about this wonderful body part – the face!

ALL *(Shouting.)* Face! Face! Face! Yeah
(Sing.)[1]
Eyes and ears and nose and mouth
Nose and mouth
Eyes and ears and nose and mouth
Nose and mouth
And hair, and chin and cheeks and eyebrows
Eyes and ears and nose and mouth
Nose and mouth

THE END

1. Sing it to the tune of "Heads, Shoulders, Knees and Toes."

This Is Your Life, Count Dracula

LEVEL OF ENGLISH: Basic

RECOMMENDED AGE: Children, ages 7 to 12

STRUCTURES:

Grammar: Simple present and simple past
Vocabulary: very simple

NUMBER OF CHARACTERS: 15 – The hostess (or host), Dracula, Dracula's mother, Frankenstein, Dracula's girlfriend, Casper, Casper's 3 uncles, 6 bats. You can add other characters, you can change the number of bats, you can eliminate characters. The number of characters is very flexible.

COSTUMES: Get ideas from Halloween stories and books about monsters.

PLAYING TIME: Approximately 5 minutes plus the song at the end

SOME SUGGESTIONS:

✸ The hostess stands in the center of the stage. When each character enters, she signals the audience to clap. After each character speaks, he or she goes to one of the sides of the stage and stands there.
✸ At the end of the sketch, when everybody sings and dances, choose a song about vampires, bats, or even a Halloween song. The song "The Batty-Bat," from Sesame Street is a nice song to use here, and can be easily found on CD.
✸ You can use this sketch for Halloween celebrations. You can also change the characters for other celebrations, like Easter ("This is your life, Easter Bunny" – use characters like the Easter Bunny, his mother, his girlfriend, his first teacher, his bunny classmates at kindergarten, etc.), Christmas ("This is your life, Santa Claus" – use characters like Santa Claus, Mrs. Claus, Santa's mother, the reindeer, etc.)

This Is Your Life, Count Dracula

CHARACTERS *Hostess*
Dracula
Mrs. Drac (Dracula's mother)
Frank (Frankenstein)
Vamp (Dracula's girlfriend)
Casper
Uncles 1 to 3
Bats 1 to 6

HOSTESS *(To the audience.)* Welcome to another edition of "This is your life!" And tonight's guest is a very famous... person? Well, he's very famous. Ladies and gentlemen, welcome Count Dracula!

DRACULA *(Enters.)* Thank you. Thank you. Thank you.

HOSTESS This is a very special night. You are going to meet some people who are very important to you. Are you ready?

DRACULA Yes. I'm a little nervous.

HOSTESS First let's call Mrs. Dracula!

(Mrs. Dracula enters, crying.)

DRACULA Mommy!

MRS. DRAC Junior!

(They hug.)

DRACULA Oh, Mom, don't call me Junior.

HOSTESS Tell us something about Count Dracula as a child.

MRS. DRAC Oh, he was so cute! He was always hungry.

HOSTESS What did he like to eat?

MRS. DRAC Blood! He's a vampire!

HOSTESS Of course... Was he a good boy?

MRS. DRAC Yes, he slept all day and only went out at night.

HOSTESS Thank you, Mrs. Dracula. *(Mrs. Drac steps aside.)* And now, here's one of your friends.

DRACULA One of my friends?

HOSTESS Yes, your best friend, Frankenstein!

(Frank enters.)

DRACULA Oh, Frankie!

FRANK Oh, Drackie!

(They hug and cry.)

HOSTESS When did you first meet?

FRANK A long, long time ago.

HOSTESS What do you do together?

FRANK We go out at night and scare people.

DRACULA Yes, we love to scare people. *(Laughs.)*

HOSTESS And now, your girlfriend. Come in Miss Vamp!

(Miss Vamp enters.)

DRACULA Oh, my love!

VAMP My dear Dracula. I love you!

(Dracula and Miss Vamp look at each other with love.)

HOSTESS Oh, what a beautiful couple!

VAMP Oh, yes. He's so charming. He's so handsome. I love him!

DRACULA Oh, I'm so happy! I think I'm going to cry...

HOSTESS No, don't cry. There's more... Here's your neighbor, Casper!

CASPER *(Enters.)* Hello, I'm your friend.

DRACULA Oh, Casper. He's a friendly ghost.

CASPER And here are my uncles.

(The uncles enter.)

UNCLE 1 How...

UNCLE 2 ...are...

UNCLE 3 ...you?

UNCLE 1 We...

UNCLE 2 ...are...

UNCLE 3 ...happy...

UNCLE 1 ...to...

UNCLE 2 ...be...

UNCLE 3 ...here.

UNCLES Boooo!!!

DRACULA They're wonderful neighbors.

HOSTESS Casper, do you like to be Count Dracula's neighbor?

CASPER I like everybody. I'm a friendly ghost.

HOSTESS Do you often visit each other?

UNCLE 1 Yes, every day.

UNCLE 2 Every night.

UNCLE 3 At midnight.

UNCLES Booooo!!!

DRACULA We have a lot of fun together.

HOSTESS And now we have a surprise for you!

DRACULA Another one?

HOSTESS Yes... Here are your pets!

(The bats enter.)

DRACULA My pets!

HOSTESS What are your names?

BAT 1 Batty.

BAT 2 Bitty.

BAT 3 Botty.

BAT 4 Batty-Batty.

BAT 5 Bitty-Bitty.

BAT 6 Botty-Botty.

BAT 1 We like Count Dracula.

BAT 2 He's very good to us.

BAT 3 He's a nice vampire.

BAT 4 He's our friend.

BAT 5 We fly together.

BAT 6 Yes, and that's great!

BAT 1 We have a surprise for you, Count Dracula.

DRACULA You do? What is it?

BAT 2 We are going to sing.

BAT 3 And dance, too.

BAT 4 Yes, sing and dance!

BAT 5 Everybody can dance.

BAT 6 Are you ready?

EVERYBODY Yes!!!

HOSTESS Thank you very much. This was "This is your life, Count Dracula!" Now, music please!

(They all sing and dance.)

THE END

Under the Sea Pirates

LEVEL OF ENGLISH: Basic

RECOMMENDED AGE: Children ages 7 to 12

STRUCTURES:

Grammar: Simple present, simple past, simple future with "will," giving suggestions with "Let's."
Vocabulary: Difference between "rob" and "steal"

NUMBER OF CHARACTERS: 6 – 3 pirates and 3 mermaids. You can use any number of characters, keeping at least 2 pirates and 2 mermaids.

COSTUMES: The mermaids can wear a tail made of paper. The pirates can wear a bandana, eye patches, and they can have a hook on one of their hands. They can also have a toy parrot on their shoulders.

PLAYING TIME: Between 5 and 8 minutes

SOME SUGGESTIONS:

- The mermaids can carry picnic baskets and sit on the floor for the picnic.
- All the characters should move their arms slowly to indicate they're under water.
- At the end of the sketch, everybody can sing a song about pirates or a song about the sea.

Under the Sea Pirates

CHARACTERS *Pirates 1 to 3*
Mermaids 1 to 3

(The pirates enter. They're wearing masks and snorkels.)

PIRATE 1 Here we are.

PIRATE 2 Yeah, finally. We're under the sea.

PIRATE 3 This was an excellent idea.

PIRATE 1 Right. We can steal a lot of things and the police won't find us.

PIRATE 2 Of course. We're under the sea.

PIRATE 3 These masks and snorkels are really helpful.

PIRATE 1 Nobody will find us here.

PIRATE 2 We're very smart pirates.

(They all laugh.)

PIRATE 3 Look, someone's coming...

PIRATE 1 Everybody hide.

(The pirates hide. The mermaids enter.)

MERMAID 1 Look! This looks like a good place for our picnic.

MERMAID 2 Yes, I like it.

MERMAID 3 Let's sit down and eat.

(The mermaids sit.)

MERMAID 1 What did you bring?

MERMAID 2 Seaweed sandwiches.

MERMAIDS Hmmm! Delicious!

MERMAID 3 I love seaweed sandwiches.

MERMAID 1 Me too. They're wonderful...

MERMAID 2 Let's eat now.

MERMAID 3 And then we can play.

MERMAID 1 Great idea!

(The pirates appear.)

PIRATE 2 Nobody move!

PIRATE 3 Hands up!

MERMAID 2 *(Shouts.)* Oh, my Neptune![1] Pirates!

MERMAID 3 Help! Help!

PIRATE 1 Quiet, girls!

PIRATE 2 Nothing will happen to you.

MERMAID 1 What do you want?

PIRATE 3 Money, jewels, gold...

PIRATE 1 Treasures...

MERMAID 2 We don't have anything.

1. This is equivalent to "Oh, my God!" since Neptune is the god of the seas.

MERMAID 3 We only have sandwiches.

MERMAID 1 Would you like one?

PIRATE 2 No!

PIRATE 3 I want one. I'm hungry...

PIRATE 1 *(To Pirate 3.)* Shut up!

MERMAID 2 Or maybe you'd like to listen to a song.

MERMAID 3 Good idea.

MERMAID 1 Let's sing girls...

(The mermaids start singing. The pirates fall in love.)

PIRATE 2 Oh, this song is beautiful...

PIRATE 3 These mermaids are beautiful...

PIRATE 1 I think I'm love.

PIRATE 2 Me too.

PIRATE 3 Me three.

MERMAID 2 It worked, girls.

MERMAID 3 It always works.

MERMAID 1 Our voices are magical.

MERMAID 2 Now these pirates won't rob us anymore.

PIRATE 1 *(To Mermaid 1.)* I love you...

PIRATE 2 *(To Mermaid 2.)* And I love you...

PIRATE 3 Let's have a party!

PIRATE 1 Let's sing and dance...

MERMAID 3 *(To the other mermaids.)* Do you think it's OK?

MERMAID 1 Of course it is.

MERMAID 2 They'll be good boys now...

MERMAID 3 And if they become bad... we'll sing again...

MERMAID 1 We are very smart!

(They all laugh. Then they sing.)[2]

THE END

2. You can use a pirate song like "A Whale of a Tale," from the movie "20,000 Leagues Under the Sea," or "A Pirate's Life's for me," from "The Pirates of the Caribbean."

Video Clip

LEVEL OF ENGLISH: Basic, very simple

RECOMMENDED AGE: Children, ages 5 to 10

STRUCTURES:

Grammar: Simple present
Vocabulary: Very simple Vocabulary

NUMBER OF CHARACTERS: 11 – a VJ, 5 singers and 5 dancers. You can change the number of singers and dancers. Just add or subtract lines accordingly. You can choose not to have any dancers – in this case ask the singers the questions about how much they practice.

COSTUMES: The VJ can wear something very colorful. You can also copy the style of a famous VJ from TV. The singers can wear leather jackets, sunglasses, or any clothes that make them look like rock singers. The dancers can wear colorful clothes. They could all wear the same color of clothes.

PLAYING TIME: Approximately 4 minutes, plus the song.

SOME SUGGESTIONS:

✷ You don't need a special setting for this sketch. The VJ can be standing, and when the band enters, they stand next to him.
✷ The VJ should look at the audience as if he were looking at a camera.
✷ You can record sounds of applause and play it when the band enters.
✷ You can have other students play the audience. They can clap when it's appropriate and shout sentences like, "Oh, they're great," "They're the best," "I love them," "C-42 is my favorite band," etc.
✷ If your students can't read yet, teach them one line at a time. Then have them repeat the whole sketch from the beginning (or as we say in theater, "from the top.")

Video Clip

CHARACTERS *VJ*
Singers 1 to 5
Dancers 1 to 5

(The VJ is alone on stage.)

VJ And now an interview with the great, fantastic, wonderful band, "C-42."

(The band enters. They wave to the audience.)

SINGER 1 Hello, everybody!

SINGER 2 It's great to be here.

SINGER 3 Yeah, it's fantastic.

SINGER 4 It's wonderful!

SINGER 5 We are very happy!

VJ Is your CD a hit?

SINGER 1 Yes, it's number 1.

SINGER 2 People love it.

SINGER 3 Everybody's singing our songs.

VJ Do you have many fans?

SINGER 4 Oh, yes, millions!

SINGER 5 Billions of fans!

VJ Do you travel a lot?

SINGER 1 Oh, yes, we do.

SINGER 2 To many places.

SINGER 3 To Brazil...

SINGER 4 To England...

SINGER 5 To Portugal, etc.

VJ There are many people in the band.

SINGER 1 Yes, there are five singers.

VJ What are your names?

SINGER 1 My name's Bob.[1]

SINGER 2 My name's Millie.

SINGER 3 I'm Chuck.

SINGER 4 Hi. I'm Billy.

SINGER 5 My name is Betty. Hi.

SINGER 2 And we have five dancers. *(Points to the dancers.)*

VJ So let's meet the dancers. What are your names?

DANCER 1 I'm Juliet.[2]

DANCER 2 My name's Peter.

DANCER 3 I'm Alice.

DANCER 4 My name's John.

DANCER 5 And my name's Maggie.

VJ Do you always dance with the band?

DANCER 1 Yes, we do.

DANCER 2 We love to dance.

DANCER 3 Our choreographies are great!

DANCER 4 People love our dance steps.

DANCER 5 They sure do.

VJ Do you practice a lot?

1. You can use the actors' real names.
2. You can use the actors' real names.

DANCER 1 Yes, we do.

DANCER 2 A lot.

DANCER 3 Five hours a day.

VJ Every day?

DANCER 4 Yes, every day.

DANCER 5 Sunday, Monday, Tuesday, Wednesday, Thursday, Friday and Saturday!

VJ Tell us about your next show.

SINGER 1 It will be tomorrow.

SINGER 2 In São Paulo, Brazil.[3]

SINGER 3 At Morumbi Stadium.[4]

SINGER 4 At 8:00 PM.

VJ So now let's watch "C-42". What song are you playing?

SINGER 5 "Rock and Roll is Here to Stay"[5]

(Music. They sing and dance.)

THE END

3. Use the name of your city.
4. Use the name of a place in your city.
5. Use a popular song at the moment.

We-have-all Grocery Store

LEVEL OF ENGLISH: Basic

RECOMMENDED AGE: Any, but specially teenagers and adults

STRUCTURES:

Grammar: Although other verb tenses appear, the focus is on the simple present.
Vocabulary: Food items

NUMBER OF CHARACTERS: 2 – George, the owner of the grocery store and Sarah, a customer

COSTUMES: George can wear ordinary clothes and an apron. The customer can wear ordinary clothes.

PLAYING TIME: Approximately 5 minutes

SOME SUGGESTIONS:

- Use a table or two to suggest the counter of the grocery store. George stands behind the counter.
- Place pictures of food items with the corresponding prices on the wall.
- You can ask students to write similar sketches that take place in other kinds of stores.

WE-HAVE-ALL GROCERY STORE[1]

CHARACTERS *George Peppers*
Sarah, a customer

(George Peppers is in the store. The phone rings.)

GEORGE *(Answering the phone.)* Hello! We-have-all Grocery Store. George Peppers speaking. Can I help you? *(Pause.)* Yes, sir, of course we sell food here. It's a grocery store – a place where you buy food – fruit, vegetables, meat, etc... Of course I'm sure. This is my grocery store. *(Pause.)* My name? George Peppers. *(Pause.)* Yes, sir, this is the best grocery store in the neighborhood – "We-have-all Grocery Store." *(Pause.)* If you want to buy food, this is the place for you. *(Pause.)* Yes, sir, our products are of the best quality. And the service is the best you can find. "We-have-all", the best grocery store of them all. *(Pause.)* You're welcome. Good bye. *(Hangs up.)*

(Sarah enters.)

SARAH Good morning.

GEORGE Good morning! May I help you?

SARAH Yes. I'd like to buy some food.

GEORGE Really? Then you came to the right place – a grocery store. In fact, the best grocery store in the neighborhood. So, what would you like?

SARAH I'd like some bread.

GEORGE Would you like a loaf of bread or would you like some buns?

SARAH A loaf, please.

GEORGE We don't have any.

SARAH OK. Then I'll take the buns.

GEORGE We don't have any, either.

SARAH You don't have any bread?

1. Inspired by the sketch "The Cheese Shop," by Monty Python.

GEORGE I'm afraid not.

SARAH Well,... that's OK... now I need some eggs.

GEORGE I'm sorry, we only have eggs on Monday.

SARAH But *it is* Monday.

GEORGE Only on the third Monday of the month, I'm sorry.

SARAH That's OK... Well... I also need some beef.

GEORGE Well, I'm afraid the truck is late. Our beef hasn't arrived yet. Don't you like chicken?

SARAH Sure. A pound, please.

GEORGE A pound?

SARAH Yes. I'd like a pound of chicken.

GEORGE But we don't sell chicken here.

SARAH So why did you ask me if I liked chicken?

GEORGE Because I like to know my customers well.

SARAH Oh, my! This is not my day, is it?

GEORGE Of course it is. Every day is customer day at "We-have-all."

SARAH Let me try some fruit. Do you have apples?

GEORGE No.

SARAH How about oranges?

GEORGE No.

SARAH Any bananas?

GEORGE No.

SARAH Pears?

GEORGE No.

SARAH Grapes?

GEORGE No.

(Getting faster and faster.)

SARAH Strawberries?

GEORGE No.

SARAH Peaches?

GEORGE No.

SARAH Lemons?

GEORGE No.

SARAH Melons?

GEORGE No.

SARAH Watermelons?

GEORGE No.

SARAH Do you have any fruit at all?

GEORGE Yes.

SARAH Good. What do you have?

GEORGE Pineapples!

SARAH Good. Give me one, please.

GEORGE The pineapples are not very good, ma'am.

SARAH I don't care. Give me one.

GEORGE They're very bad, ma'am. They're spoiled.

SARAH They're spoiled?

GEORGE They're spoiled. They look bad, they smell bad and they taste bad.

SARAH I don't mind. I love pineapples anyway. Give me one, please.

GEORGE If you insist... *(Looks under the counter.)* Oh no!

SARAH What is it now?

GEORGE The dog ate all the pineapples.

SARAH The dog? Ate the pineapples?

GEORGE I'm sorry, ma'am. That dog loves fruit, you know.

SARAH This is not a very good grocery store, is it?

GEORGE Of course it is. It's the best grocery store in the neighborhood. I think I can say it's the best grocery store in town.

SARAH What's so good about it?

GEORGE Well... it's so... clean.

SARAH Of course it's clean. It's empty. No bread, no eggs, no meat, no fruit, no vegetables.

GEORGE Oh, oh, oh. I didn't say we don't have vegetables.

SARAH Do you?

GEORGE Well, we have...

SARAH *(Interrupting.)* No, no... let me guess. Do you have lettuce?

GEORGE Not lettuce, no.

SARAH Cabbage?

GEORGE I sold the last head this morning.

SARAH Tomatoes?

GEORGE No.

SARAH Peppers?

GEORGE Yes?

SARAH OK. Give me a pound, please.

GEORGE A pound of what?

SARAH A pound of peppers.

GEORGE Oh, I'm sorry. I thought you were calling me. My name's George Peppers.

SARAH *(Getting angry.)* Carrots?

GEORGE No.

SARAH Onions?

GEORGE No. Onions make me cry.

(Getting faster and faster.)

SARAH Potatoes?

GEORGE No

SARAH Asparagus?

GEORGE No.

SARAH Green beans?

GEORGE No.

SARAH Celery?

GEORGE No.

SARAH Broccoli?

GEORGE No.

SARAH Caulifllower?

GEORGE No.

SARAH I'm gonna ask you one last question. Is there any food in this grocery store?

GEORGE Ma'am, this is the best grocery store in town.

SARAH Answer my question. Is there any food in this store?

GEORGE No. But we do have excellent service. *(With a big smile.)* May I help you?

SARAH I'm getting out of here. *(Exits.)*

GEORGE *(Looking out of the door, very friendly.)* Have a nice day! Good bye! Come back soon! Don't forget to tell your friends! *(To the audience.)* I do my best, but some customers are so difficult to please.

THE END

What Do You Want to Be?

LEVEL OF ENGLISH: Basic

RECOMMENDED AGE: Children, ages 7 to 12

STRUCTURES:

Grammar: Simple present, want + to + verb
Vocabulary: occupations

NUMBER OF CHARACTERS: 12 children. You can use any number of children

COSTUMES: Ordinary clothes

PLAYING TIME: Approximately 5 minutes

SOME SUGGESTIONS:

✷ The setting can be anything. The children can be in a park, sitting on the floor or they can be in a room (use chairs as couches).
✷ The miming that the students have to do doesn't have to be perfect. On the contrary – it will be funnier if it's not very good.

What Do You Want to Be?

CHARACTERS *Children 1 to 12*

(The children are together. Child 10 is thinking.)

CHILD 1 Let's play a game.

CHILD 2 Good idea.

CHILD 3 Yes. I like games.

CHILD 4 Me too.

CHILD 5 What game can we play?

CHILD 6 I don't know.

CHILD 7 Any ideas?

CHILD 8 No.

CHILD 9 *(To Child 10.)* Do you have any ideas?

(Child 10 doesn't answer.)

CHILD 11 *(To Child 10, waving his/her hand.)* Hey! Hello!

CHILD 10 *(Noticing the other children.)* Yes?

CHILD 12 What are you doing?

CHILD 10 I'm thinking.

CHILD 1 Thinking? About what?

CHILD 10 About my future.

CHILD 2 What do you mean?

CHILD 10 I'm thinking about my job.

CHILD 3 What do you want to be?

CHILD 10 I don't know.

CHILD 4 *(Having an idea.)* Hey, everybody!

CHILD 5 What?

CHILD 4 I have an idea.

CHILD 6 What is it?

CHILD 4 Let's play the "What do you want to be" game.

CHILD 7 What kind of game is that?

CHILD 4 It's a guessing game.

CHILD 8 A guessing game?

CHILD 4 Yes. We mime the occupation and the others try to guess it.

CHILD 9 For example?

CHILD 4 For example. I want to be a... *(Mimes a pilot.)*

CHILD 10 What's that?

CHILD 11 I know! A pilot!

CHILD 4 Yes. I want to be a pilot.

CHILD 5 My father's a pilot.

CHILD 6 Really?

CHILD 7 My turn now. I want to be a... *(Mimes a doctor.)*

CHILD 8 A teacher?

CHILD 7 No. I want to be a... *(Mimes a doctor.)*

CHILD 9 A police officer?

CHILD 7 No. Pay attention. I want to be a... *(Mimes a doctor.)*

CHILD 10 I know! I know! A doctor!

CHILD 7 Yes. I want to be a doctor.

CHILD 11 Me too. My mother's a doctor. I want to be a doctor, too.

CHILD 12 My grandfather's a doctor. But I want to be a... *(Mimes a clown.)*

CHILD 1 What's that?

CHILD 2 An English teacher at Super English School?[1]

(They all laugh.)

CHILD 12 No. I want to be a... *(Mimes a clown.)*

CHILD 4 It's difficult.

CHILD 5 I don't know.

CHILD 12 Concentrate. I want to be a... *(Mimes a clown.)*

CHILD 6 This is funny.

CHILD 8 A clown! Clowns are funny!

CHILD 12 Yes, that's it. I want to be a clown at the circus.

CHILD 9 I want to be a... *(Mimes a police officer.)*

CHILD 11 That's easy. A police officer.

CHILD 1 And I want to be a... *(Mimes a firefighter.)*

CHILD 2 An English teacher at Super English School?

(They all laugh.)

CHILD 1 No. I want to be a... *(Mimes a firefighter.)*

CHILD 10 An acrobat?

CHILD 1 No. I want to be a... *(Mimes a firefighter.)*

CHILD 3 A soldier.

CHILD 1 No. I want to be a... *(Mimes a firefighter.)*

CHILD 3 I give up.

CHILD 4 Me too.

1. Use the name of your school.

CHILD 5 It's very difficult.

CHILD 1 Do you all give up?

CHILDREN Yes.

CHILD 2 I want to be a firefighter.

CHILDREN Oh...

CHILD 2 My turn now. I want to be...

(Child 2 mimes a very funny and exaggerated job.)

CHILD 3 A clown?

CHILD 2 No.

(Child 2 continues miming.)

CHILD 4 A farmer?

CHILD 2 No.

CHILD 5 A firefighter?

CHILD 2 No.

CHILD 6 A doctor?

CHILD 2 No.

CHILD 7 What is it?

CHILD 2 You have to guess.

CHILD 9 I give up.

CHILD 9 Come on, tell us.

CHILD 2 You have to guess.

CHILDREN What is it?

CHILD 2 Do you give up?

CHILDREN Yes!

CHILD 2 I want to be...

CHILDREN Yes?

CHILD 2 An English teacher at Super English School.

(They all laugh.)

THE END

Plays, Level of English and Recommended Age

PLAY	LEVEL OF ENGLISH	RECOMMENDED AGE
An Acting Class	Lower intermediate	Teenagers and adults
At the Bookstore	Basic	Teenagers and adults
Beauty Sleep	Basic	Children and teenagers
Cinderella	Basic	Any
Confusions	Basic	Teenagers and adults
Count it Higher	Basic	Children, ages 6 to 12
Don't Leave Me	Intermediate to advanced	Teenagers and adults
Dry Bones	Basic	Children (ages 8 and above) and teenagers
Fashion	Basic	Children (ages 8 and above) and teenagers
Going to the Zoo	Basic	Children, ages 7 and above
Little Red Riding Hood	Basic	Any
Love Class	Basic	Children ages 7 and above
Mr. Ache – Version 1	Basic and Intermediate	Teenagers and adults
Mr. Ache – Version 2	Basic and Intermediate	Teenagers and adults
Mr. Ache – Version 3	Basic and Intermediate	Teenagers and adults
On Old McDonald's Farm	Basic, very simple	Children, ages 7 and above
Please Mr. Postman	Intermediate	Teenagers and adults
Rabbit News Program	Basic	Children, ages 5 to 12
School for Fish	Basic	Children (ages 10 and above) and teenagers
The Big Bad Wolf's School	Intermediate	Children ages 8 to 12
The English Student	Basic	Teenagers and adults
The ETs	Basic, very simple	Children, from 5 years old
The Fight	Basic	Children, ages 6 and above
The Joe Puppy Program	Basic	Children, ages 8 and above
The Presidential Debate	Lower Intermediate	Any
The Rabbit Family Game – Version 1	Basic, very simple	Children
The Rabbit Family Game – Version 2	Basic	Children
The Rich Old Man	Lower intermediate	Any
The Scarecrows	Basic	Children, ages 8 and above
The Secret	Basic, very simple	Children, ages 5 to 12
The Traffic Jam	Basic, very simple	Children, ages 6 to 10
The Under the Sea Hospital	Basic	Children (ages 8 and above) and teenagers
The Wheels on the Bus	Basic, very simple	Children, ages 5 to 8
Think of Your Fingers	Basic	Any
This Is Your Face	Basic	Children, ages 7 to 12
This Is Your Life, Count Dracula	Basic	Children, ages 7 to 12
Under the Sea Pirates	Basic	Children ages 7 to 12
Video Clip	Basic, very simple	Children, ages 5 to 10
We-have-all Grocery Store	Basic	Any
What Do You Want to Be?	Basic	Children, ages 7 to 12

Este livro foi composto na fonte Proforma
e impresso em maio de 2005 pela Prol Editora Gráfica Ltda.,
sobre papel Offset 75g/m².